# The Culture Industry

## The arts in urban regeneration

*Edited by*

DEREK WYNNE

*Department of Social Science*
*Manchester Polytechnic*

Avebury

Aldershot · Brookfield USA · Hong Kong · Singapore · Sydney

Published by
Avebury
Ashgate Publishing Limited
Gower House
Croft Road
Aldershot
Hants GU11 3HR
England

Ashgate Publishing Company
Old Post Road
Brookfield
Vermont 05036
USA

A CIP catalogue record for this book is available from the British Library and the US Library of Congress



ISBN 1 85628 287 2

Printed and Bound in Great Britain by
Athenaeum Press Ltd., Newcastle upon Tyne.

THE CULTURE INDUSTRY

To Jenny, Mat and Kirsti

# Contents


| | | |
|---|---|---|
| Acknowledgements | | vi |
| Introduction | | vii |
| 1 Cultural Industries | *Derek Wynne* | 1 |
| 2 Cultural Quarters | *Derek Wynne* | 13 |
| 3 Television: A Strategy for Expansion | *Haydn Shaughnessy* | 24 |
| 4 The Popular Music Industry | *Steve Redhead* | 42 |
| 5 Local Government and Cultural Policy | *Justin O'Connor* | 56 |
| 6 Issues in Education and Training | *Linda Dockery* | 70 |
| 7 Urban Regeneration and the Arts | *Derek Wynne* | 84 |
| 8 The Economics of the Culture Industry | *Howard Hughes & Chris Gratton* | 96 |
| Appendix I Cultural Production Tables | *Howard Hughes* | 109 |
| Appendix II Cultural Consumption Tables | *Chris Gratton* | 117 |

# Acknowledgements

*The Culture Industry* was written as a consultancy report by a team of researchers at the Centre for Employment Research (CER), Manchester Polytechnic. The report was commissioned by Greater Manchester Economic Development Ltd., and North West Arts and was funded by these organisations together with: Central Manchester Development Corporation; Wimpey Homes; Seward and Cruichshank Ltd.; EGS Design; Lander Alarms; Dunlop Heywood.

The authors would like to thank the staff of CER, especially Bernard Leach, Director, Dave Nicholson and David Gibbs for their help and support during the research period. Thanks are also due to Alan McGarvey and Paul Hammond formerly of GMED Ltd., and Josephine Burns, formerly Director of North West Arts, together with those individuals from the companies and organisations above who formed a steering group for the period of the research programme. Thanks also to Carolyn Beecham, Steve Campbell and Alan Tice for their work in the data collection and its processing. A personal note of thanks is also due to my colleague Phil Mole, office companion and longtime friend, for his consistent help and support. Finally we would like to thank all those who responded to our enquiries with patience and good humour in The Culture Industry of Greater Manchester.

# Introduction

Unlike traditional texts *The Culture Industry* is a consultancy report written to a specific brief. As such we feel a note of explanation is warranted concerning the production of the text. Each of the first six chapters begins with a short introduction, followed by a set of recommendations which are then discussed in further detail. The layout of the text is, therefore, directly related to the recommendations made at the beginning of each chapter. Headings within each of the chapters, and points arising from the discussion which have a direct bearing on specific recommendations, are highlighted in the text for ease of reference.

Chapter one argues for a strategy designed to further develop the economy of the culture industry. This includes development loans, managed workspace, marketing and distribution services to assist the growth of cultural producers.

In chapter two we examine the development of cultural quarters and indicate their importance in providing for a sense of 'place' in downtown locations. The creation of such quarters, is, we believe, a necessary ingredient in creating an 'ambience' which further encourages the use of cultural facilities by both resident populations and tourists alike. Additionally, such quarters also provide for further commercial investment and provide an identity important in the attraction of inward investment.

Chapters three and four examine two of Manchester's most successful cultural industries, television and pop music. We indicate a strategy for expansion in the television industry which centres around the recent developments in distribution technology and we suggest ways in which wider commercial interests can be encouraged in this industry. For the development of the pop industry we make a series of recommendations which include investment in marketing and distribution, as well as performance and production.

The role of the local authorities in the formulation of cultural policy is examined in chapter five. Here we recommend a series of steps that could be taken in the development of a strategy which emphasises the importance of the arts to both local economic development and the generation of civic pride. Such an emphasis is not intended to undermine the role of the arts as cultural service provision, but rather to affirm the economic importance of such provision.

Chapter six outlines the role of educational and training institutions in arts related employment. Our recommendation for an education and training forum is intended to indicate how important such education and training is if the industry is to develop and expand.

Development in the arts and cultural industries elsewhere is examined in chapter seven of the report. Here we show how other towns and cities have adopted an arts led urban regeneration strategy by defining the arts as part of the urban infrastructure. Such regeneration strategies have included: creating opportunities for physical improvement, extending provision for cultural producers in the form of studio workspace, and providing enhanced opportunities for cultural consumption.

The final chapter of our study reports on the surveys which were undertaken of cultural production and consumption. The former provides an indication of the current state of cultural production in Greater Manchester, documenting the size and economic importance of the culture industry to the region. The latter provides an analysis of the economic importance of the arts consumer, indicating the importance of the arts to the wider economy. This chapter also provides an indication of Greater Manchester's arts economy in relation to others elsewhere. While we believe that our figures provide a favourable indication of the arts economy in this region we wish to point out that comparisons are invariably fraught with difficulty, given the problems associated with survey sizes, time periods, measurement techniques and the like.

The text is deliberately, and perhaps somewhat provocatively titled, 'The Culture Industry' in order to emphasise the role which the arts play in the economy: a role which places the arts in the mainstream of economic life. We define the culture industry as including *all* forms of activity associated with what is traditionally understood as art *and* popular culture. This includes the live performance and *singular* artistic production, together with the recorded and *reproduced* productions in the audio and visual media.

Such a definition allows for an examination of a variety of forms associated with the transmission of meaning and avoids the problems associated with the traditional distinctions between 'high' and 'popular' culture, and the live and reproduced performance or art work. We believe that the arts gain nothing from this artificial separation produced by distinguishing their form.

The context of our report can be placed in the debate surrounding the observed decline in traditional industries and in the efforts to provide for economic regeneration through the development of the service industries. Over a period of years now, many regional economies where primary manufacturing industry had once played a major part, have sadly suffered a spiral of decline. It is not our intention to dwell, or indeed document this decline. Nevertheless it is perhaps worth pointing out that our estimates of the annual turnover and employment levels of The Culture Industry in the Greater Manchester region should be seen in the context of similar figures from other sectors. For example the textiles industry in Greater Manchester employed 23,600 people according to the 1987 Census of Employment. We estimate that at a minimum level the culture industry employs over 10,000 people. Gross output in the textile industry of £743 million (figures from the 1985 Census of Production) compares with our estimates of £343 million for the culture industry in 1988. Clearly the culture industry provides an important source of both employment and wealth for the region in an area of the economy which has expanded significantly in recent years. The growing importance of the retail sector with which the cultural industry is so closely allied can be gauged from the fact in retail distribution there were almost 100,000 employees in Greater Manchester recorded in the 1987 Census of Employment. Our report notes the importance of this link in chapter eight, where we examine the 'non-arts' expenditure of arts consumers, which we estimate to be some £87 million in 1989, a figure worth approximately £18 million to the local economy and generating almost 5,500 jobs. Similar linkages also exist, of course, with the regions tourist industry. Each year over 10 million overnight stays are made in Greater Manchester by tourists. By 1988 tourism was estimated to be worth £218 million to Greater Manchester, a figure in which the culture industry undoubtedly plays a significant part ( L&R Leisure Consultants, 1988).

However in addition to analysing the importance of the arts and cultural industries in the Greater Manchester economy, our brief asked us to note those areas where strategic intervention could be of benefit to the wider community. The report provides a series of strategies for North West Arts, development agencies, local authorities, educational and training institutions, community arts organisations, and commercial enterprises. We believe that the strategies we recommend will further stimulate all sectors of the arts and cultural industries. In addition we have examined the emergence of arts led urban regeneration strategies elsewhere in an effort to indicate how the city and towns of the region can employ similar initiatives themselves.

We would wish our report to be considered primarily as a case study and examination of Greater Manchester's cultural industry, rather than as an overt comparison with the economic importance of the arts elsewhere. Certainly we would hope that it adds to the body of knowledge already gained from other investigations, however we believe that little would be gained from a simplistic comparison of the size of the culture industry in different locales.

Although our recommendations have been produced with regard to the development of the arts and cultural industries in Greater Manchester, we are confident that the ensuing discussions will be of relevance to both policy makers and academics. The interest in 'arts led' urban regeneration strategies and the forging of public - private sector links in the development of these strategies requires a reconsideration of the relationships between both culture and the economy, and private and public investment alike. As we indicate in the text, a number of cities and urban regions have begun to develop such strategy in both North America and Europe, and a number of conferences in both the academic and policy-making fields have devoted attention to these issues.

In conclusion, while our emphasis is on the economic benefits that can be wrought, we are acutely aware of the social and educational importance of the arts to the wider population. The confidence, general well being and personal development to be gained from an involvement in the arts and cultural activity cannot be overstated, and we would wish to affirm our own accordance with such a view. However, we also believe that the arts can, and should be, a daily part of people's lives and would argue therefore, that they reside within the wider community associated with that everyday life, rather than existing as an appendage to it. As such, the arts are inextricably bound to both the economic and wider social life of the community. They *deserve* to be examined for the economic benefits that they provide, rather than be seen to reside in some exclusive arena outside of everyday experience. It is in this sense that we argue for the development of the arts to be seen as a form of investment rather than subsidy: an investment which provides both an economic return of some considerable size, and an investment in the quality of life to be enjoyed.

# 1 Cultural industries

## *Derek Wynne*

### Introduction

This chapter examines strategies for the development of the culture industry in Greater Manchester. It begins with a short discussion of our definition of the culture industry, its growing economic importance, and the wider role that it can play in the socio-cultural life of the community.

We define the culture industry as including all forms of activity associated with what is traditionally understood as art and popular culture. This includes the live performance and singular artistic production, together with the recorded and reproduced productions in the audio and visual media. We have adopted this broadest of definitions because of the increasing "crossovers" between different forms of cultural activity, and because we believe that the culture industry and the benefits which flow from it, both economic and social, gain nothing from an artificial separation produced by distinguishing their form. Importantly we reject the distinctions which regard culture as limited to a definition of art as 'high culture'; which distinguish between commercial and non-commercial consumption and production of cultural provision and products; and which define cultural policy simply as the provision of leisure and arts facilities. We believe that a wider definition is important in order to promote the conceptual leap necessary if the arts are to take their proper place in the new economy upon which successful regeneration strategies need to be based. A new economy which demands investment in the arts (culture industry), education and training, and a high technology infrastructure. However, for the purposes of this section of the report, such a broad definition is intended to act more as an orienting theme to our recommendations, rather than to initiate discussion as to what categories of activity such a definition would include. Consequently our recommendations, their potential development, and our discussion of initiatives taken elsewhere, should be seen as indicative rather than exclusive.

The growing economic importance of the culture industry can be seen in the fact that in 1986 the net balance of trade for Great Britain's publishing industry was £550 million; recorded music £495 million. Non-broadcast video production turnover in 1987 has been estimated to be in the region of £300 million annually. Recent estimates on the Leisure Industry are that it currently accounts for approximately 25% of consumer spending, estimated in 1986 to be some £58 billion. Our own research estimates that turnover in the culture industry in Greater Manchester for 1988-9 is approximately £343 millions and that this sector employs over 10,000 people. Even when we exclude the major broadcasting organisations, direct turnover exceeds £100 millions and the sector employs over 6,500 people. Indirect turnover and employment, is, of course, considerably greater. A detailed analysis of the economic importance of the arts and culture industry to Greater Manchester is provided in section eight. Clearly this sector is one of considerable importance to the Greater Manchester economy.

With further investment there is considerable room for expansion, and our recommendations are intended to provide an indication of how increased investment in this sector will lead to further increases in business growth and employment opportunities. The particular development potential in the music, audio-visual production and telecommunications industries are examined in detail in sections three and four of our report. Here we are primarily concerned with establishing a framework for the development of cultural production in more general terms and we examine opportunities for: investment in cultural production; property led mixed development, including managed workshop/studio and exhibition space; marketing and distribution initiatives. In addition to the above we also wish to point out the importance of investment in both education and training if the culture industry is to attain it's full economic potential in the region. To that end we devote section six to these issues, while recognising their related importance to this particular section.

**Recommendations**

Our principal recommendations for the continued development of the culture industry are:

- the establishment of a Development Loans Fund for small businesses and organisations working in the culture industry;

- the provision of mixed, multi-occupancy, studio-workspaces with managed business services for artists and cultural producers. Consideration should be given to the property led development of integrated managed workspace/exhibition space in cultural quarters;

- the creation of a limited company or similar organisation to progress the development of studio workspace for artists and cultural producers. Such an organisation would play an important role in working with property developers, local authorities and others in ensuring that the property requirements of cultural producers were catered for;

- the creation of a limited company or similar organisation to provide marketing and distribution services for artists and cultural producers in Greater Manchester. Currently Arts About Manchester (AAM) performs this role for a consortia of venues. We believe a similar role could be performed on behalf of cultural producers;

- an integrated telecommunications network to be established for cultural producers and organisations associated with the promotion and development of the arts and culture industry in Greater Manchester. Such a network would further encourage the "crossovers" in cultural production that we have identified, and further enable cooperation between cultural producers;

- the development of a communicative database and published directory of artists and cultural producers in Greater Manchester to be used in promotion/marketing in addition to its function as a trade directory. A similar database to be created for exhibition space, galleries, venues and museums.

**Cultural Industries: Background**

*Development Loans for Cultural Producers*

Establishing a development loans fund for cultural producers would provide one way of stimulating production and enterprise activity in this sector. Our research indicates that cultural producers fail to conform to the traditional models of the small business, and therefore find it difficult to raise the necessary capital for growth. As such they are often financially ill equipped to successfully develop their activities on a scale that would ensure their success. We believe two principal reasons are responsible for this; an inadequate understanding of cultural production by financial organisations, and the failure of cultural producers to appreciate the nature of commercial activity.

Our survey of cultural producers discovered that many of them felt that financial institutions were unaware of the commercial potential of the culture industry. Respondents were asked to express their opinions about commercial lenders of finance. An overwhelming majority (86.5%) considered that such lenders were less aware of the nature and requirements of the culture industry than they were of manufacturing industries. Further details of our survey appear in section eight of this report.

However, while recognising the importance of short courses developed by North West Arts aimed at encouraging a more "businesslike" approach amongst artists and cultural producers, we would suggest that financial institutions become more responsive, not just to the needs, but also the commercial opportunities of cultural production. Therefore we recommend the creation of a development loans fund to assist cultural producers in developing their commercial activities. Greater Manchester Economic Development Ltd., (GMED), in cooperation with North West Arts (NWA), would appear to be the ideal organisation to administer such a fund on behalf of a consortium of major financial institutions. In addition to assisting individual cultural producers, such a fund might also assist, along with public sector provision, the development of related business services in marketing and distribution.

Clearly a set of criteria would need to be developed regarding definitions of cultural production, together with some assessment of the individuals and organisations working in these fields. We feel that NWA, the regional arts association, would be best equipped to develop these criteria. Given GMED's considerable experience in the management of capital funds, together with their brief to encourage economic development, and to establish links between the public and private sectors, we believe that they would be the ideal organisation to administer such a programme.

*Studio Workspace*

Our recommendations regarding the provision of studio workspace facilities should be seen as integral not only to the development of the culture industry, but also as an essential part of an arts led urban regeneration strategy. The advantages of such provision are that it would provide much needed facilities for cultural producers together with 'mixed' development opportunities in which cultural production and consumption would co-exist. Such a mix would also facilitate the increasing 'crossover' taking place in different areas of cultural production. Finally, studio workspace facilities could also include managed business services for cultural producers on a collective basis.

We feel such development is particularly necessary given that there is some evidence to suggest that cultural producers currently and previously located in the city centre will need, or have been required, to vacate premises. At the same time, by establishing mixed facilities for cultural production and consumption the artist is brought closer to his/her public; thus improving prospects for consumption and establishing the artists position as a member, rather than an esoteric observer, of the wider community. By locating cultural producers from different artistic disciplines in shared workspace developments greater opportunities for both artistic and commercial "crossovers" are encouraged and the sharing of business services would remove some of the business management responsibilities which many artists are ill equipped to respond to. We would add that in this sense many "own account" artists are effectively running small businesses, and therefore face very similar problems to those faced by small businesses generally. The development of managed workspace for small businesses is, therefore, well suited to the needs of these small cultural producers. Locating cultural producers in mixed developments allows possibilities for both cross subsidy, i.e. rental for artists workspace could be subsidised with rentals obtained from more overtly commercial activities, and for the utilisation of areas of buildings where available space is not suited to other commercial enterprises.

The importance of "crossover" in cultural production is indicated in our survey finding that just under half (46%) of the respondents engaged in more than one activity of cultural production. Crossover was particularly common in the media arts and visual arts, drama and dance, and design/craft and the visual arts. Through the provision of studio workspace for different types of artist this "coming together" of different artistic forms can be encouraged. Nowhere is this more apparent than in popular music and fine art. The successful production and promotion of records often involves a variety of cultural producers which include video and sound engineers, graphic artists, textile designers, as well as the musicians themselves. Similarly in fine arts the traditional distinctions between canvas, materials sculpture, video, film and still photography are also beginning to disappear as artists explore new mediums.

The survey also provides an indication of the length of time that respondents had been engaged in their artistic activities. The relatively high percentage of newcomers amongst individuals is perhaps a reflection both of a rapid turnover in these sectors, and an indication of the vitality of cultural production in the region. Information was also sought about the premises used by the respondents for offices, production, performing, display, workshop areas and for rehearsal and storage. Not all respondents necessarily had a need for all three categories and others may have used the one premises for several purposes. Use of part of own residence was common amongst those in the visual arts 29.4%, and design/craft 39.1%. Although the majority of respondents considered that their premises were adequate or very adequate (Table 4), this situation was reversed for rehearsal/storage facilities. This aspect of dissatisfaction was apparent for nearly all categories or respondent.

In addition to our questionnaire survey we also carried out a series of interviews with cultural producers in a variety of fields which lead us to conclude that the provision of managed workspace with shared business services would be an important step in further facilitating greater commercial success in this sector. This point is reinforced in our discussion of cultural quarters where we recommend the provision of mixed development cultural production and consumption facilities (see chapter two).

The concept of managed workspaces is not new. There are precedents of a sort in the commodity exchanges of the Victorian era or the Inns of Court in London. There are a number of reasons however for the recent upsurge of interest in the concept. These include first, a concern with the nature and type of premises available to small businesses, particularly the need for flexible letting arrangements for small firms. Second, concern about the number of redundant industrial and commercial buildings in the inner city areas, together with a new awareness of the potential for reusing such buildings. Third, the emergence of new forms of working practice, including the emergence in different forms of the "working community" idea, whereby small firms in the same or complementary sectors cooperate in sharing a building and services: eg craft centres, fashion design centres, arts centres. Lastly, an increasing awareness that many one-person, "micro enterprises" have neither the time, resources, nor skills, to become proficient in every aspect of business operation. They therefore require access to, for example, marketing and accounting provision on-site. ie incorporated in workspace provision.

The acquisition of appropriate premises together with problems in obtaining planning permission are often cited as problems experienced particularly by small businesses, which, of course, characterise many cultural producers. The need for inexpensive rental premises is a problem experienced by small businesses generally. However, it would be especially useful to assess the particular premises requirements of businesses in the cultural production sector in order to identify any specific difficulties with premises. The following examples show how these issues relate to managed workspace developments.

In our analysis of developments elsewhere in chapter seven of this report we discuss the work of Workshop and Artists Studio Provision Scotland Ltd., (WASPS), together with the development of Newcastle Arts Centre. WASPS is a non-profit making company established in 1977 with support from the Scottish Arts Council and provides workshop and studio provision for artists in a number of towns and cities throughout Scotland. The Newcastle Arts Centre (see chapter two) is a joint development of the local authority and voluntary sector which provides work and studio space in an arts centre in downtown Newcastle. Both of these developments are further examined later in this report.

*Hackney Enterprise Workshop* is a small workspace established for the benefit of disadvantaged minority groups. The scheme was established by the London Borough of Hackney, and has been funded by the Borough through the Urban Programme. The facility has a total lettable area of 3000 sq ft, divided into 14 units each of 200 sq ft. It has a 100% occupancy level and the 13 client firms are all run by local residents. A total of 35 people are employed, and about half the firms are run by women. All except one of the client businesses (a secretarial firm) are in cultural production, with a predominance of firms in fashion and textile related areas. The scheme is targeted primarily at starter businesses and clients are encouraged to leave after one year. This is generally agreeable to them as by this time they usually need more space.

The workshop provides an extremely supportive environment for its occupants. Firstly there is the shared machinery which is available to licensees and casual users free of charge - a silk screen printing machine, a stationery printing machine, a cutting machine, a three thread sewing machine, button hole machines, a cutting table, computer equipment and a steam press. There are two communal working areas in addition to a small meeting room and tearoom. Then there are communal vehicles, for which a charge is made according to use:- a delivery van, a trailer and an exhibition van. There are four members of staff, all employees of Hackney Borough Council:- full time manager, full time financial adviser, part time caretaker and part time secretary. Seven of the client businesses are clothing-related; the remainder are a picture framer, a secretarial firm, a postcard printer and a handtools repairer. Twenty three firms have moved on from the workshops. Four of these have gone out of full time employment and 19 have continued trading. A major problem however is in finding suitable premises for firms once they leave these starter units.

Within the Greater Manchester area a number of councils have begun to address these questions. For example Bolton MBC has built workshop developments especially geared to the needs of ethnic minority businesses and Rochdale MBC has advanced plans to develop a Fashion/Textile Design Centre.

Manchester City Council has assisted certain developments, with both financial and non-financial aid; Cariocca Enterprises and WorkSpace North West.

*Cariocca Enterprises* is a Company Limited by Guarantee managed by a Board of twelve, comprising nine community representatives recruited through the West Indian Organisations Coordinating Committee, two Councillors and a representative of the Manchester City Council economic development Committee. Its primary aim at present is the development of a large, purpose built Managed Workspace facility of 117 units in Ardwick, scheduled for completion in March 1990. The facilities on offer will include secretarial support and accountancy services, reprographics facilities, together with a permanent in-house business consultancy service. The workspace will be open to all inner city businesses but will be particularly targeted at the Afro Caribbean community. The main target group are identified through a threefold categorisation. First, those who have been failed by the education system and who wish to create employment opportunities for themselves through the pursuit of entrepreneurial activity. Second, those who have previously tried to set up in business but have failed due to lack of skills and experience. Third, existing small businesses which have the potential for expansion but which are unable to do so due to lack of resources and skills.

It is a further stated aim of Cariocca that surpluses built up in the course of its activities will be used to 'Fund any groups whose aim is to combat disadvantage in the community'. In the longer term they aim to develop retail outlets - community owned in the same way as the workspace facility - primarily for the use of the same categories of business as those targeted for the workspace.

*WorkSpace (North West) 23 New Mount Street* is a managed workspace project which has been developed by Workspace (North West) in conjunction with Manchester City Council. The premises provide office, studio and workshop space together with a range of business support services. These services include: twentyfour hour access throughout the week; central reception; secretarial facilities; telex, fax and photocopying; cafe and kitchen areas. Space is available in units which range from 100 to 1600 square feet and can be rented with only one month's notice. The policy of Workspace NorthWest Ltd is to provide easy in/easy out terms for small companies and micro businesses. Although 23 New Mount Street is not specifically intended for cultural producers it is interesting to note that a number of cultural producers have recently located there. These include; Be Bop Cassettes; Scam Promotions; and Sunset Radio; together with a number of others in the fashion, design, craft and publishing sectors. Networking and mutual cooperation has already developed amongst some of these organisations and there is clearly scope for the provision of further developments along these lines.

Both of these initiatives display characteristics which go beyond basic workspace provision to offer shared, and often cooperatively managed, facilities which many "micro enterprises" (particularly in cultural production) increasingly require. The implications of the above discussion are that the suitability of premises is more a function of the sector and size of operation of the business; the suitability of premises is directly related to the extent of provision of ancillary back-up business support services.

*Marketing Initiatives*

A major problem faced by all small businesses, but particularly by cultural producers either in "micro enterprises" or self employed, is the problem of marketing - individual businesses too often lack the resources or expertise to maximise the marketing of their goods and services. One solution to this problem lies in the development of marketing co-operatives. A marketing co-operative is quite simply a company with a board of directors but where each director is a representative of a member firm of the co-operative and the marketing co-operative itself is non profit-making. Its function is to help its member firms increase their profits by expanding their sales. Members are usually firms in the same or related sectors. The marketing co-operative has long been a feature of the UK farming sector but the idea has not made much headway in other sectors of the economy. This is in stark contrast to the situation in Italy where it is held that the success of the Italian small business sector owes a great deal to the proliferation of marketing co-operatives.

The organisation of small business networks in certain areas of Italy provides a useful model by which to envisage the organisation of cultural producers in the Greater Manchester region. The area of Italy concerned is that known as the Third Italy, between the undeveloped south, and the large scale industrial regions of the north west (Milan, Turin, Genoa). It has also become known by its central regional focus, Emilia-Romagna. This area is characterised by high quality production in districts comprised of a number of similar and complimentary small firms, linked to each other by formal and informal networks of co-operation and co-ordination. This allows such firms to embark on a process of flexible specialisation, a strategy dependent on a level of co-operation geared towards a coordinated response to a fragmented, specialist market. This model of co-operation within autonomy, of a highly designed product produced by a skilled workforce, could be seen as a potential model for coordinating cultural production, distribution and marketing for Greater Manchester's cultural producers. The success of the Emilia-Romagna approach depends on the development of close co-operation between firms, allowing each to specialise and to have ready access to the full range of requisite business services. Activity is then co-ordinated through consultative networks, both formal and informal.

Informal networks amongst Manchester's Cultural Producers are well developed in certain areas of activity, but it is increasingly recognised that there need to be more formal links between them, providing information, advice, and business services such as marketing and distribution. The Italian Consorzio provides an example of one such formal network. The Consorzio facilitates inter-firm networking through the establishment of an association of enterprises designed to provide a common service. A typical Consorzio would provide services in three related areas of business management. First, those services traditionally associated with managed workspace provision including office management, accounting and secretarial services. Second, services related to distribution and marketing such as representation at trade fairs, export promotion, sales missions and market research. Third, services associated with reducing production costs such as the funding of new tecchnology, training, and organising the bulk buying of production materials. Consorzio membership fees are supported by various national and regional economic development offices. Such Consorzia allow small businesses in complimentary sectors access to services previously restricted to large corporations without losing the initiative and organisational flexibility associated with the small firm. They can also co-ordinate product lines and specialisation such that firms do not produce the same product and compete over price. It is clear that such a model has direct relevance for the culture industry in capitalisation funding, the management of workspace provision and administration, and the provision of marketing and distribution services.

One British example of a marketing and distribution service for the fashion industry is Black Country Fashions, a clothing marketing co-operative in Wolverhampton. This co-operative was launched in April 1989 with 12 members. the members were selected from the members of the Wolverhampton Association of Fashion Houses by consultants from Wolverhampton Business School and the West Midlands Clothing Resource Centre after the Black Country Development Agency had identified the need for a mini-clothing complex in the area. A shop, in the centre of Wolverhampton, was provided by the local authority for six weeks as a showcase to attract business from both the public and the fashion industry. After its first month it had reached a turnover of about £1000 per week. Future plans for the co-operative include establishing itself in a permanent shop, finding a full-time marketing agent, encouraging more designers to join and producing a catalogue.

*Integrated Premises and Marketing*

The case studies quoted above indicate that the provision of adequate physical premises cannot be considered in isolation from the provision of ancillary business services eg secretarial and administrative support, shared use of plant and equipment. A further example of a marketing initiative in the fashion industry is the Nottingham Fashion Centre. While this example is not actually integrated into a workspace provision, it does nevertheless show what sort of marketing services could be provided in an integrated workspace/marketing initiative in that particular industry. As such, it should provide an indication as to the ways in which initiatives in Greater Manchester might develop. An outline of what an integrated workspace/marketing development might look like would thus be provided by a combination of the example of the Hackney Enterprise Workshop and the following example of the Nottingham Fashion Centre. Nottingham Fashion Centre aims to improve contact between local clothing manufacturers and potential customers with the objective of generating more trade. Its initial focus was a programme of exhibitions featuring locally designed and locally manufactured garments. These were held in the well-equipped showrooms at the centre, to which buyers from national and international clothing companies were invited. Later more emphasis was given to taking displays of local products to national trade fairs. The centre maintains a register of local production capacity and specialist producers; it has a library of yarns and fashion forecasts to which designers and manufacturers refer; it rents out its showrooms to individual firms for private shows and training sessions; and it provides general and specialist business advice. The centre was initiated by the Nottingham City Council and is funded through the Urban Programme.

Whilst the promotion of Trade Exhibitions has had a limited success, the Information and advisory Services have been used extensively. Briefly these comprise business advice with finance and production, display services including exhibitions and promotional literature, a fabrics library, a register service of firms and individuals offering specialist production skills.

A Department of Environment report concludes the following lessons for good practice from this example:

> The experience of Nottingham Fashion centre highlights for all sector marketing initiatives the importance of understanding clients' needs and "getting under the skin" of the industry. To overcomcollective wariness it is essential to win the trust and support of local businesses at an early stage and to promote private sector participation in the venture. Only later can initiatives hope to change traditional patterns of working. (HMSO, 1988).

The case study also illustrates the need to be adaptable in trying out different approaches after disappointing results were achieved and the value of sectoral approaches in developing knowledge of local industry. As has been suggested above, this example is potentially of great value in considering appropriate assistance in marketing for cultural producers, particularly those in the fashion sector. When considered in the context of appropriate workspace provision it also opens up the possibility of developing an integrated managed workspace and marketing centre, geared to other enterprises in cultural production.

*Marketing Services*

A further consideration is the provision of marketing services for both new start-ups and longer established businesses. The need for marketing support is explicitly recognised in all the case studies quoted above. However in a sectorally specific managed workspace development, marketing services can be fully integrated into the whole project. The fashion industry is one obvious sector for such an initiative - although the same principles can be applied to other sectors of cultural production, particularly in areas which enjoy considerable "crossover".

In Greater Manchester one agency which providing marketing support is Arts About Manchester (AAM). AAM is a marketing consortium originally developed by NWA. It has been recently launched as an independent organisation in its own right and currently employs a full time marketing officer. AAM's membership is based primarily on theatres, concert venues and galleries in the Greater Manchester area.

Organisations pay a differential subscription, according to their size, for marketing and print distribution services. We believe that the continued development of such services is essential to the successful promotion of the arts in the region and would argue for a similar service to be introduced for those working in areas of the cultural industries such as pop music, crafts/fashion and small scale audio-visual production. We feel that both AAM and any proposed distribution and marketing agency for other cultural producers should engage in research to refine their marketing activities, and should consider the use of the new information technologies discussed below as a means to improving these.

*Marketing: Communications Technology and the Culture Industry*

When we began our research on this project we were advised by a number of people that the anarchic nature of cultural production would provide us with a series of problems. Because areas of artistic activity are so diverse, and artists so "fiercely independent" it was suggested that any attempt to monitor and account for their activities would prove especially difficult. Although these representations are undoubtedly true in certain areas of artistic endeavour, we have, at the same time, discovered a series of inter-relations in a variety of artistic fields. In particular we note the "crossover" between the audio-visual, pop music, and fashion industries. Similarly we would point to other "crossovers" associated with two factors. First, those that link the retail sector and cultural production in music, fashion, crafts and fine art. Second, those between the consumption and production of cultural products; emphasising that cultural consumers of what one might term auditorium or exhibition events tend also to be the consumers of other cultural products. Given the importance of such "crossovers" in the fields of both cultural production and consumption we recommend their encouragement through the establishment of low cost communications technology. The availability of such facilities as a communications network to arts organisations, and "commercial" cultural producers would further encourage "crossover" both artistically and commercially, and provide arts organisations with information on each others activities. At the same time this communications technology would also serve a vital function in the development of marketing and distribution of cultural products, and in the establishment and maintenance of the proposed "trade directory" of cultural producers in Greater Manchester. Although our report on the Television Production Sector examines the emergence of new technologies of a greater magnitude than those referred to above, we believe that the introduction of "low cost" technologies in arts organisations and managed workspace facilities would have positive effects on the culture industry.

We have stressed the importance of the "crossover" links between the different sectors of the culture industry and between producers, retailers and consumers. Building on the formal and informal networks already established is an important step in the generation of new or expanded networks and new forms of cultural production and consumption. A particular need is to provide initial access to such networks to those groups at present largely excluded.

*Manchester Host Computer*

To facilitate networking it is proposed that use be made of the Manchester Host computer communications and information system. This scheme is being developed by Manchester City Council, and feasibility studies are under way at the present time, with implementation planned for 1990. There are a variety of ways in which the culture industry could participate in this system, which will be locally-based, technologically sophisticated but with low entry costs for any organisation wishing to participate. The Manchester Host Computer will give computer users access to (via a modem and at the cost of a local telephone call), a range of "on-line" services including electronic mail, bulletin boards, conference facilities, document transfer, databases, telex/fax services, on-line translation, interactive training and electronic publishing.

Cultural producer organisations could initially be encouraged to purchase the necessary equipment, with the possibility of grants for those based in Manchester, from the City Council's Innovation Initiatives grants scheme. Such organisations would then be able to join the Host network and explore the potential of the new communications technology. It is important however that a "critical mass" of cultural producers be established in the region, to enable networking to develop. To this end the possibility should be explored of leasing space on the computer specifically for the culture industry which then could be specifically marketed at producer organisations. We would suggest that North West Arts would be the relevant organisation to explore the possible benefits of developing such a user group and of becoming involved in the implementation phase of the Host computer to ensure that potential spinoffs for the culture industry are explored.

**Conclusion**

This section of the report has made a number of recommendations which we believe will enhance the development of the culture industry in Greater Manchester. These recommendations centre around three strategies. Financial provision through the introduction of cultural development loans. Managed studio, workspace and exhibition provision through property led mixed development initiatives. Shared marketing and distribution for cultural producers.

Clearly, these recommendations relate to other sections of our report and are particularly relevant to the sections on Education and Training and Local Authority Cultural Policy. They should also be seen as an introduction for, and complimentary to, some of the recommendations contained in the chapters concerned with television production and the popular music industry. Our emphasis on "crossover" amongst cultural producers, and the relationships between cultural production and consumption also have important implications for the development of cultural quarters which are examined in chapter two.

# 2 Cultural quarters

*Derek Wynne*

## Introduction

Our study has examined the development of cultural quarters in a variety of towns and cities. Further details of this examination are given in section seven of our report. Although we believe that the development of cultural quarters can achieve similar goals in both the surrounding towns and the city centre, it is inevitably the case that the diversity and magnitude of cultural quarter development will be greatest in the city centre. We begin with a discussion which provides the rationale for our recommendations for the city centre. This is followed by a discussion on the development of cultural quarters for the towns of Greater Manchester. Of course, much of what we have to say regarding city centre development is equally applicable to the surrounding towns. The concluding section of the report provides a discussion of the nature of the cultural quarter and examines the development of Harbourfront in Toronto, and the Newcastle Arts Centre, noting the similarities between these developments and some of our own recommendations.

### *City Centre Cultural Quarters*

The rationale for our recommendations centres around questions concerning: location; the applicability of mixed use development for cultural quarters; the nature of arts-led urban regeneration; the role of cultural tourism. We believe that there are at least two areas of the city which commend themselves to the development of cultural quarters, in addition to Chinatown where consideration should be given to development which reflects this communities needs. At the same time we recognise that current development, notably that associated with the activities of the Central Manchester Development Corporation, and that of the Manchester City Council will inevitably effect the creation of such quarters. Consequently we offer below two possible areas for consideration, not withstanding our previous comments. The two quarters that we refer to above are physically located in:

(i) the area of the city from Oxford street at the intersection of Portland Street to the north and west towards Castlefield. This area already incorporates many of the city centres premiere entertainments including The Cornerhouse, Palace Theatre, Green Room, Hacienda, Free Trade Hall, Opera House and G-Mex, together with a number of bars, and cafes. In addition, this area has planned developments for a new concert hall housing the Halle, and the proposed Festival Marketplace Shopping in the Great Northern Goods Wharehouse. One could consider the area bounded to the east, by Oxford Road, the Town Hall and Quay Street. To the North the area is bounded by Castlefield, and eventually, the river. Given the existing facilities mentioned above, together with those planned viz the Concert Hall and Festival Market Place retail, and the intention to attract residential development, this area becomes a prime candidate for activities associated with the cultural quarter. Additionally it should be noted that the Strategic Development Initiative highlights the way in which the river Irwell and canal systems provide the potential for a natural link between this area, the Pomona Dock, Trafford Park's proposed developments and those currently underway at Salford Quays. The development of an arts led urban regeneration strategy in these areas could be one way of providing a conceptual link to these currently distinct locations.

(ii) The area to the south and east of the Arndale Centre in central Manchester, extending to the inner relief road and south towards Piccadilly. Although this area does not contain the same amount of cultural facilities as that referred to above, it does nevertheless contain some which are a significant part of what one might term Manchester's young and alternative "scene", namely, Afflecks Palace, an "alternative" clothing and fashion retail multi-occupancy building of national prominence on this "scene": The Band On The Wall a jazz and contemporary music venue of international reputation: the recently opened, Dry 201 - a venture associated with the Factory organisation examined in the report on the popular music industry. In addition to the above the Manchester Craft Centre is located in this area, as is Sunset Radio and Bop Cassettes. Regarding future development, one might consider this area as bounded by the proposed International Trade Centre and Piccadilly Village to the south.

Our decision to recommend the development of two areas rather than one is a reflection of the changing dynamics of both the modern city, and the patterns of cultural consumption and production associated with it. In short, people move around the city in different ways, viewing it as a social as well as physical space. Our research leads us to believe that both of these areas of the city are used for the cultural facilities which they offer, and that continued demand for both cultural consumption and production are great enough for the city to contain cultural quarter development in both of these areas. Such development possesses the further attraction of widening the relatively small city centre to both the east and west, and of encouraging related development in tourism, other commercial activity and housing development.

Our recommendation for mixed use development reflects the nature of the relationship between cultural production and cultural consumption. Such production work in film, fashion, textile and clothing design, in addition to the fine arts and crafts is increasingly a part of the consumption process. The relatively high value - added nature of the production process in the cultural industries, requires that the cultural producer retains as close a link as possible to the point of cultural consumption. In addition, the nature of the cultural production process is invariably "friendly" to the consumption process. Such "friendliness" is the principle reason behind the "festival market place" concept of linking "crafts" activity to wider consumer retail, and of providing "arts entertainment" activity in retail settings. Such developments recognise that shopping, particularly in the city centre, is increasingly seen as a leisure experience. A second feature which commends such development is that of the "crossover" between cultural producers. Such "crossover" is nowhere more evident in the fashion, audio-visual and music industries where cultural producers in one sector are increasingly employed in the other (see chapter one).

For the above reasons we recommend mixed use developments that "cross" both the consumption and production processes, and that recognise the inter-relations between different cultural producers. In arguing for the recognition of facilities for the arts and cultural industries as part of the infrastructure of urban regeneration we wish to stress the role that such facilities play in creating the ambience and therefore demand for city centre developments in retail, other commercial, office and residential accommodation. Arts led strategies have become one of the principal means by which urban regeneration has been accomplished in other parts of the world. These strategies are examined in more detail in section seven of the report. Numerous examples of such strategies exist in North America, Toronto and Boston, and Britain's best known example, Glasgow. Such strategies have tended to focus on cultural consumption, but as we indicate above, could also incorporate cultural production facilities. Indeed, recent evidence from Toronto has encouraged this city to make further resources available to its cultural producers, in the form of studio/workspace facilities.

Given the relatively meagre economic resources of many small cultural producers (see chapters one and eight), it is inevitably the case that, like many other small businesses, they will be unable to compete in a property market as buoyant as that in city centre Manchester. However, given their undoubted importance to the success of urban regeneration schemes it is imperative that strategies for such schemes take account of the nature of these economic resources. Consequently, just as consideration is being given to affordable housing projects such as those in Whitworth Street, it is essential that similar consideration is given to the provision of studio/workspace for cultural producers, together with the provision of facilities which extend opportunities for cultural consumption. It is in this sense that we argue for a treatment of the arts and cultural industries as part of the infrastructure of successful urban regeneration. Such claims are based on a definition of such provision as necessary infrastructure investment, rather than a definition of such provision as subsidy. Our recommendation that a cultural quarters trust be established to promote, market and administer cultural animation programmes provides one way in which public private sector investment can assist the process of arts-led urban regeneration in the creation of cultural quarters.

The Strategic Development Initiative (SDI) produced by Manchester, Trafford and Salford Councils could provide the framework for the development of cultural/entertainments quarters for these local authorities. The SDI also incorporates areas currently under the control of both Trafford Park and Central Manchester UDC's. As such it provides the ideal framework for cooperation between all of these organisations and could therefore be used as the starting point for all major regeneration projects in this area, and also serve as a useful model to those outside. While it is not necessary to conceive a master plan which would demarcate particular types of provision for each separate area, it is nevertheless desirable that organisations attend to each others regeneration efforts.

Just as the Toronto Harbourfront's lakeside location (see below) has become the principal feature in its development, the river and canal sides and basins could become the principal orienting features in the development of this area. Indeed the human scale of the river, it is relatively small and therefore easily crossed by pedestrians, makes Riverside and the surrounding canal systems the ideal location for the development of cultural/entertainments quarters. Through the initial development of cultural and entertainment provision along Riverside, including investment in the cultural industries, not only would cultural tourism increase, but property development in the surrounding area could orientate toward such provision. Such orientation could then be used to maintain and extend the cultural facilities offered on Riverside. In this way cooperation between the private and public sectors could assist and support the Cultural Sector Trust in ways similar to those created in both Toronto and Boston. The trust could be given a brief similar to that of the Harbourfront, Toronto as regards the management and provision of cultural and entertainments activities for Riverside. Essentially this brief would be to manage and encourage the development of cultural and entertainment activities for the local population and visitors by providing regular and frequent events on Riverside and the canal basins incorporating all aspects of the arts and entertainment industries. Such an organisation, in addition to planning such events, and encouraging provision by others, could also provide a valuable expertise in assisting the local authorities and UDC's development projects in the area. With waterfront land at a premium valuable contributions, financial and otherwise, could be made available for the landscaping, public art/sculpting, and entertainment/artistic developments which would be necessary for Riverside's successful regeneration. In examining this part of the study brief support from developers has been canvassed and obtained from most of those companies with development proposals in the locations referred to above.

*Cultural Quarters in Greater Manchester's Towns*

Much of what has been said above, is, of course, relevant to the town centre's of Greater Manchester. Our discussion of Newcastle's Arts Centre and City Centre Dublin (see below) is specifically addressed towards possible development in the town centres. Indeed we note similar developments in Greater Manchester, notably the proposals for Derby Hall in Bury. Other examples which could usefully be examined can be found in St Helens (The Citadel), and Burnley (Burnley Mechanics).

For the region's towns we recommend the development of multi-use Arts Centres, located in central areas. This recommendation is based on our examination of developments elsewhere, particularly Newcastle and Dublin (see chapter seven) together with consideration of the Policy Studies Institute Report, (PSI, 1987). Such centres can accomplish a number of desirable features to encourage the arts and cultural industries in establishing a cultural quarter. First, they contribute to the use of downtown areas, particularly in the evenings, thus contributing to the vitality of such areas in both economic and social spheres. Second, they provide facilities for "communities of interest" in developing arts activities and enable the development of professional and semi-professional artists. Third, they provide for a "one stop" location for arts services and major provision. In addition we believe that the success of the Sports Council's "Sport For All" campaign owes much to the development of the multi-use sports centre which has formed one of the main planks of the Sports Council's recent activities.

As with such sports centres consideration must be given to the demands of the community over and above the traditional definitions of artistic practice. Outreach and education for art should respond to a communities demands and is therefore a necessary, but secondary requirement in comparison to provision. The cultural quarters trust would take on the same role as that envisaged above, seeking to provide for cultural animation programmes via support from both local government and the local commercial sector in the town centres in which such quarters were located. Although the surrounding towns are unable to offer the degree of cultural consumption available in the city centre, or indeed the degree of cultural production facilities, nevertheless a number of the regions towns do possess a town centre structure containing retail and cultural facilities. These, together with town centre "arts centres" could provide such towns with cultural quarters, allowing them access to the benefits, albeit on a reduced scale, available to the city centre.

*Further Development*

Our research leads us to believe that no single local authority department could progress such developments in isolation. Centrally located arts centres would impact across a number of departments including Cultural and Leisure Services, Economic Development, Planning, Tourism and Education. Consideration needs to be given as to how such departments can cooperate in order to promote the development of such centres. In addition to the above, effective transportation into town centres from outlying areas would be a necessary requirement for such provision. We believe that the local authority executive needs to consider the following issues. First, ways in which an integrated interdepartmental approach to further development can be taken. Second, possible funding opportunities involving public/private sector cooperation. Third, finding ways of using the expertise of both Greater Manchester Economic Development Ltd and North West Arts in proposals to develop such quarters.

**Recommendations**

This section of our report has been developed from an extensive examination of cultural quarter development in towns and cities elsewhere in the British Isles, Europe and North America. These developments are examined in further detail in section seven of our report. Here we concentrate on those issues most pertinent to the development of cultural quarters in Greater Manchester. We recommend that:

- Cultural quarter development in the city centre should be considered in the light of the Strategic Development Initiative produced by the Manchester, Salford, Trafford Local Authorities, in cooperation with the English Tourist Board.
- Consideration be given to the development of cultural quarters, rather than one cultural quarter which would contain all of the city centres cultural and entertainments opportunities.
- The plans of both development corporations should be coordinated, and special attention given to those of CMUDC given its city centre location.
- For the town centres in Greater Manchester we recommend that they consider the development of multi-use arts centres in their own town centres. Such arts centres to contain opportunities for:
    - community/multicultural arts and outreach work;
    - professional and semi-professional workspace/rehearsal studios;
    - management and administrative offices together with business services available to both professional and voluntary associations;
    - linkage with other town centre leisure, arts and retail facilities thus contributing to the development of a "critical mass" of such facilities.
- While recognising the increased possibilities within the city centre, we recommend that both town and city centre cultural quarters comprise facilities for cultural consumption and cultural production including property led mixed use developments. This requires that attention should be given to the location of mixed use facilities which would incorporate performance, exhibition and workshop studio space for the cultural industries.
- The necessity of joint public private sector cooperation should be recognised and attention given to developers plans to incorporate arts related facilities into proposed developments.
- The expertise of North West Arts and GMED should be employed in any attempts to develop such quarters. Local authorities and development corporations should seek to ensure that any proposed development incorporating the arts and cultural industries is examined by these organisations at an early stage, so that recommendations appropriate to the development of the arts and cultural industries in Greater Manchester can be considered.
- GMED, in its role as the economic development organisation for the

Association of Greater Manchester Authorities should be party to any cultural quarter development plans in order to ensure even development throughout the region.

In concluding our recommendations we wish to stress that attempts to develop such facilities be understood and planned for as part of the infrastructure of urban regeneration; that cultural quarters trusts be established to promote, market and administer cultural animation programmes; the importance of cultural tourism should be recognised, catered for and aggressively marketed.

**Cultural Quarters: Background**

As stated above, considerable attention is given to the development of cultural quarters in other towns and cities elsewhere in this report (see section seven). Here we briefly examine the concept of the cultural quarter, point to it's use as an aid to urban regeneration, and provide details of some recent examples of cultural quarter development. For the reader interested in exploring these and other developments in more detail we recommend an examination of chapter seven.

A cultural and entertainments quarter can be defined as that geographical area which contains the highest concentration of cultural and entertainment facilities in a city or town. Most of the "great" cities of the world possess such quarters which have evolved over time and have longed provided both accommodation and work opportunities for actors, musicians, dancers, artists, and, more recently, those working in film and the electronic media. It is in such quarters that the greatest concentration of theatres, cinemas, studios, galleries, concert halls, bookshops, restaurants, cafes and bars are found. They become, in essence, the cities avant garde heart, and provide, with their "critical mass" a meeting place for residents and tourists alike to participate in the cultural and entertainment nightlife of the city. Paris has its left-bamk, Montmartre and Beaubourg, London its Soho and West End, New York has Greenwich Village, Soho, and more recently the mid-west side. Such quarters have grown symbiotically over long periods of time and have a spatial, socio-economic and political history to their development.

However, more recently a number of cities and towns have begun the process of developing and planning such quarters, and in some cases, notably Boston, New York and Toronto, attempting to protect them from development inimical to their existence. As part of this study we have examined the attempted development of cultural quarters in a number of cities and towns in the UK, elsewhere in Europe, and North America, in an effort to suggest ways in which both Manchester City Centre and the surrounding Greater Manchester town centres might consider such developments themselves. Recent development of the cultural quarter has taken place in an effort to encourage urban revitalisation through three inter-related strategies. First, residential development of no longer used industrial premises to encourage population growth in downtown areas. Second, new forms of retail development to combat the growth of "out of town" shopping. Third, measures to aid the development of the city centre 'night time' economy. In short, cultural quarters have become one of the main strategies of arts-led attempts at urban regeneration.

Our discussions with a variety of personnel in cities where such quarters have been, or are being developed, namely, Toronto, Boston, Rotterdam and Glasgow provide support for our recommendations. Although further details of such development can be found in section seven, Developments Elsewhere, we feel it worthwhile to review here the development and operation of three such quarters, namely Harbourfront Toronto, that being developed in Newcastle City Centre, and the City Centre Dublin, given that our recommendations regarding the creation of Cultural Quarters and Cultural Quarters Trusts bear some resemblance to these.

*Toronto Harbourfront*

The Toronto Harbourfront development is a Canadian federal government initiative, begun in the early seventies, but one which has only in the last ten years begun to take shape. Although its role is not directly equivalent to that of the UDC's, certainly its activities could be said to be somewhat similar to those proposed by the CMDC, given the latter's central location, unlike other UDC's. This gives the CMDC a role which it sees as concentrating on light commercial/office, residential, leisure and cultural development, rather than on the industrial development associated with the other UDC's. The mandate prescribed by the federal government for Harbourfront includes: to develop Harbourfront as Toronto's central urban waterfront; to develop Harbourfront as a public space; to develop Harbourfront in ways that account for its special location, conditions and history; to achieve financial self-sufficiency. The above has been accomplished by a recognition of the economic importance of the arts and cultural industries in urban regeneration and from the beginning of the project the corporation recognised the need to provide for a variety of cultural events and activities in order to attract the Toronto public and tourists to the area, in the recognition that private development would inevitably follow in the form of retail, hotel and residential development. Consequently the corporation has been able to convince potential developers that the arts, rather than being understood as subsidised activities, are an essential part of the successful regeneration of the area. In essence they have become a part of the infrastructure costs of successful urban regeneration. Rather than being understood as an extra burden on developers, or a subsidised activity, they are seen as being as necessary and as important as other forms of infrastructure such as transportation and utilities provision.

The corporation, has a series of powers viewed with suspicion by some in local politics, ie like CMDC it is not a democratically elected local organisation, and has a number of powers related to planning, compulsory purchase etc. However most would know concur that the role which it has developed and the development which it has produced on the waterline, does offer both Torontonians and tourists a series of cultural and leisure opportunities which blend well (mostly) with the work undertaken by Toronto City Council in this area of activity. Importantly the land on which Harbourfront operates is federal land, and therefore monies accruing from the sale and leasing of this land form part of the budget for the development and subsidy of the cultural programmes offered at Harbourfront. As such some of this land is offered for sale and lease by Harbourfront for private sector development in specific areas of activity Hotels, shopping, residence. Capital accumulation from land sales and rents from leases are then used by Harbourfront to reinvest in cultural programmes. Consequently although Harbourfront has a different brief to the CMDC, it does share some similar features to the CMDC in that its task has been to attract mixed use development of a retail, residence, touristic, and cultural nature. The major difference is that the Harbourfront Corporation owns the land on which it operates.

*Newcastle City Centre*

Two approaches can be discerned in Newcastle's arts led attempts at urban regeneration. The first relates to proposals to create the West Village in the west end of the city, incorporating the restored Tyneside Theatre. The second is the creation of Newcastle Arts Centre which has seen the conversion of a group of derelict buildings into a mixed development which houses media workshops, an exhibition space and a studio theatre. The council's role in the development of the arts centre has been significant, as has its contribution to the restoration of the Theatre Royal, the Tyne Theatre, Opera House and Tyneside Cinema.

However the proposed West Village is primarily a flagship project of the Newcastle Initiative, a primarily private sector body. Its plans for the Village include the creation of a cultural district which will include both speciality retail, along the lines of the festival shopping concept, together with some components of the cultural industries, probably crafts, fine arts and fashion design and residential accommodation. This development can be seen as a direct result of the initiative taken in the development of Newcastle Arts Centre.

*Newcastle Arts Centre*

The arts centre provides an excellent example of the way in which arts led developments can be seen as investment assets in addition to publicly subsidised services in that it was primarily through this initiative that private sector interest was generated in the West Village. The centre contains the following facilities:

- an exhibition hall
- 250 seat theatre
- media centre
- 15 artists studios and workshops
- office space
- restaurant and bar
- central courtyard for exhibition and meeting place.

Shop units are currently being developed where artists and crafts people will be able to retail their cultural productions.

This centre provides an excellent example of how the voluntary sector and local authority can develop initiatives which not only provide facilities for mixed use cultural consumption and production, but also stimulate similar activity within the private sector. Further details of this development are provided in section seven of this report.

*City Centre Dublin*

The City Centre Dublin is the trading name of the Grapevine Arts Centre Ltd which receives funding from the Arts Council of Ireland. Grapevine is a company limited by guarantee, initially created in 1974. At the present time there are fourteen directors of the company which is, in essence, a non profit organisation. The directors and members receive no financial dividends. The Centre is located in a former art college which has been renovated for use as an Arts Centre, incorporating facilities for both cultural consumption and cultural production. It's activities can be broken down into a series of activities which include; training and education, job creation and entertainment. In addition the centre plans to develop managed workspace for cultural producers. Financial support for this development has come from public, private and voluntary sources including; the Arts Council of Ireland, U2, the Youth Employment Agency, Dublin Corporation, and Allied Irish Finance.

The building contains three floors, each of which is dedicated to specific activities. The basement provides four rock rehearsal studios for young bands to develop their music. On the ground floor is a performance space with 224 seats surrounded by a restaurant, bar, box office and reception. The first floor provides a series of studios dedicated to architectural design, photography, drama and dance. The second floor provides over 2,000 square feet for the development of enterprise units in the cultural industries, together with four studio workshops for lease to cultural producers. In addition, service facilities for cultural producers and other arts organisations are provided in the form of a design studio, a print workshop and a public relations agency specifically geared to arts and community organisations. Finally two international artists studios have been provided to encourage artists from abroad to develop their work in Dublin.

Like Newcastle Arts Centre, City Centre Dublin provides an excellent example of the way in which the arts and cultural industries can provide not only an important service to the community, but can also aid the process of urban regeneration by providing a focus for the establishment of other commercial ventures complementary to the cultural industries and therefore assisting in the creation of the cultural quarter.

**Conclusion**

Essentially cultural quarters can be described as those "downtown" areas of towns and cities where entertainments and cultural facilities are located. It is argued that a "critical mass" of such facilities, when located alongside others such as commercial, retail and residential, i.e. mixed use areas, brings positive benefits which can include both economic and wider social benefits, such as the development of the retail sector and increased feelings of safety in night time 'downtown' locations. Evidence from developments elsewhere suggest that cultural quarters are an effective and appropriate way to stimulate urban regeneration. Such development can incorporate facilities for both cultural consumption and cultural production, and need not be confined to a single physical area of the city. As we have noted above, Manchester city centre could accommodate two such quarters catering for different, yet complimentary, aspects of the arts and cultural industries. However we believe that mixed use development is a neccessary feature of such quarters which must incorporate residential opportunities as well as facilities for both cultural consumption and production. Only in this way can a 'critical mass' of facilities be developed.

# 3 Television: A strategy for expansion

*Haydn Shaughnessy*

**Introduction**

Television broadcasting is expanding and becoming more international. Like all industries it will be affected by the 1992 Single Market, though, unlike other industries, the language barrier will protect English broadcasting from full European competition.

In the United Kingdom the debate over the future of broadcasting still centres on the issue of quality vs expanded choice. Well established broadcasters argue that the Government's White Paper on Broadcasting could lead to an irreparable loss in programme standards. However the debate has yet to focus on the positive aspects of the White Paper. The White Paper proposes a number of means of expanding the distribution of television programmes. It is important for an area such as Greater Manchester to consider what can be gained from these policies.

The production and distribution of television programmes in the area is still dominated by the ITV/BBC duopoly. The Government regards this as a barrier to economic growth, and has designed the White Paper to break this duopoly down, and provide lower costs of entry to this expanding industry. New distribution technologies - cable, satellite and microwave technology offer a way of complementing and expanding the broadcasting system, and in the long run of creating many more jobs. However the conventional broadcasters are skilled at projecting a powerful case for the retention of the status quo.

Development agencies in the North West will be able to work in conjunction with the established broadcasters, Granada and BBC North West, on some of the proposals made in this report. However the logic of expansion is that the duopoly organisations will lose a share of their influence. It would be contrary to the wishes of proposed legislation that further development of the industry is controlled either by the BBC or ITV companies. Local agencies cannot depend on the duopoly for further expansion, and must therefore face the problem of intervening in an industry in which they are inexperienced and perhaps overawed by technical terminology.

At some stage in the development of a media policy, it is essential for Greater Manchester to look abroad, at developments in Europe. The UK market is dominated by London-based independent production houses and London based satellite consortia. Europe presents a different market and the possibility of new alliances. However the European scene is complex and open to a variety of international influences and defensive policy initiatives. Competition from the U.S.A. will become an increasingly important factor, determining the cost and content of programmes and Government and E.C. policy towards television broadcasting. UK and European broadcasters will be faced with the option of buying in cheap U.S. programming or radically reducing their own programme production costs. Whilst domestic quota legislation will give the European industry some protection, European producers and broadcasters will continue to enter co-production agreements in order to realise the benefits of a European, as opposed to domestic, market. These international factors will have a growing impact on the independent production sector in Greater Manchester, if that sector aspires to a significant role in this expanding industry.

The promotion of small independent production companies is often quoted as a means of expanding local production. However the independent production sector in Greater Manchester lags behind some other regions. Manchester's independent production sector is relatively young. It is by no means strong enough to enter overseas markets, or the market for satellite programme production. Much of this "new" independent industry is in fact a displacement of personnel from Granada TV and BBC North West. It therefore represents only a minimal level of "expansion". The BBC and Granada are both reducing production costs by shedding staff.

Markets in the UK are already dominated by London producers. The room for expansion in the local production sector is small unless Greater Manchester is able to seize the opportunities presented by new distribution technology. Whatever the merits of the local independent production sector it cannot expand, significantly, without new forms of distribution. Local producers would be expected to make use of local television production facilities. Some companies do not do this, claiming that local facilities are inadequate and overpriced. There is also a claim that local facilities cannot match the professionalism of London facilities houses. As a result some local companies prefer to travel to London to edit their programmes. Rectifying this problem will be difficult in a staunchly independent environment.

A new terrestrial channel - Channel 5 - is due to begin in 1992/3. Channel 5 will not be allocated to one franchise holder but will be divided into two or more separate time-bands - a breakfast franchise, night time franchise and peak hours franchise. Its coverage is expected to be limited to about 70% of the population. Many cities can be expected to lobby for Channel 5 to be allocated to their area in the expectation that it will provide a substantial impetus to local television production. However it will face unprecedented competition from national and international programmes distributed via satellite and cable; and possibly from local programmes distributed by microwave. Channel 5 will not give the kind of impetus to programme production that many people expect. Whilst we recommend that the local agencies lobby for part of the Channel 5 franchise to be based here, we do not recommend that local agencies place too much faith in this as a means of expanding the local industry.

Technological innovation is a feature of programme production, as well as programme distribution. One such innovation is the development of High Definition Television. The EC is sponsoring research into a European standard for High Definition Television. The BBC is lobbying for the EC to fund an HDTV studio in the UK. G.M.E.D. and other agencies can lobby to ensure that the BBC, if it is successful, bases its new studio in Greater Manchester.

New distribution technology not only offers an opportunity for expanding television programme distribution - and therefore expanding production. The technology is capable of improving the communications capabilities of all sections of local industry and commerce. For this reason we have made several recommendations for ensuring that these technologies are adopted enthusiastically.

The cost of satellite communications is expected to fall significantly over the next five years due to deregulation and increased competition. Satellite communications will become more widespread, and more familiar to business. Cable, satellite and microwave technology can be used not only to stimulate media production. These technologies can also be used to stimulate other forms of cultural production. Local live events and artistic production could find a local showcase in cable TV, and an international showcase through satellite television.

**Recommendations**

The specific recommendations we make are divided into three headings:
Promoting new distribution technologies
Enhancing the local production base
Enhancing the communications capabilities of local industry and commerce.

*Promoting New Distribution Technologies: Cable, Satellite and Microwave*

A Communications Forum should be set up. It would need to be co-ordinated by a local organisation which has the trust of the business community and the local authorities. G.M.E.D. could consider taking on this role. The Forum would consider the following tasks in promoting the new distribution technologies:
- realising the potential of fibre optic cable by commissioning feasibility work for a Manchester Cable Franchise. Such work should also consider the commercial feasibility of a microwave network linking fibre optic islands in the Greater Manchester region to a city centre cable system
-investigating demand for satellite communications facilities. Promoting development in satellite TV would help justify investment in satellite

communications for other sectors of the economy. It is possible to conceive of the North West making a contribution to satellite TV output in collaboration with cultural producers in continental Europe. Satellite channels tend to be built around specific "themes". We suggest four possible themes:
- a Comedy channel;
- a Live Event Cultural channel, to which local cultural producers contribute, and which might run in conjunction with cultural production in the regions of Europe;
- an Educational channel;
- an Ethnic Minority channel.

Any one of these themes could be used as a way of encouraging more local arts and culture onto television. This would stimulate local arts production and local television production.

Consideration might be given to an application for one or both of the two remaining BSB Channels, though we caution against the possible losses involved. As a major shareholder in British Satellite Broadcasting, Granada TV might wish to encourage a franchise bid from Greater Manchester.

The Government plans to privatise the television distribution network. Existing distribution technology can be used for different purposes, including:
- teletext distribution
- data distribution
- TV programme distribution.

A privatised network implies that new profit centres, and new centres of influence will develop. These trends need to be monitored.

A five year communications development plan for Greater Manchester could be drawn up which would co-ordinate development in fibre optic cable, microwave distribution and satellite communications. Such a development plan could be employed in:
- Attracting Investors. A useful model for the use of media planning as an instrument of inward investment already exists: The Cologne Media Park provides a technological infrastructure for the arts and cultural industries and for local business. It is now a major aspect of Cologne's inward investment strategy.
- The formation of a North West Satellite User's Group which would bring together interested parties. The "User Group" model has precedents in Continental Europe. It can be likened to a club, in which potential satellite users combine their demand and effectively reduce the costs of purchasing satellite time. The "Club" model also allows users to share the cost of promoting their services.

*Enhancing the Local Production Base*

We believe the only viable form of long term intervention, to promote the local independent production sector, is to promote new forms of distribution. Planning for the independent sector should be framed in these terms. However a strategy for this sector applicable in the short term should include:
- investing in improved local independent production facilities
- examining the BBC's plans for a prestigious High Definition Television studio. Attracting such a project to the area would help lay a foundation for

new production facilities in the 1990s;
- an audit of local facilities paying particular attention to the need for improved computer graphics facilities. Some work has already been done on this in the COMEDIA A-V Strategy;
- promote a Channel 5 franchise bid - perhaps through the Communications Forum;
- expanding Film and Video Animation - a recognised area of excellence;
- management training courses for facilities and production companies, possibly funded through the EC's MEDIA project;
- a programme of high quality skills training is needed if the local facilities sector is to realise its potential. G.M.E.D. and North West Arts can make a case for substantial investment in state-of-the-art technology for training purposes. In a creative industry, experimentation is a key factor in skills development. Consideration should be given to the development of a Media Centre which would act as a centre of excellence in film and video arts, with the emphasis on advanced forms of training;
- G.M.E.D. in collaboration with North West Arts and A.G.M.A. could appoint a Media and Communications Officer to liaise with the European Community's MEDIA project - ensuring that Greater Manchester companies have access to MEDIA funds. The same officer should make contact with small independent producers in the European Community and investigate the scope for collaboration. Manchester could take the lead in forming a European Regional Producers Association, in order to build links between regional producers in Europe;
- given the 1992 Single Market arrangements, attention should also be paid to the growing demand for "dubbing" and "subtitling" foreign films, and English films for the foreign market. This is a small industry which will inevitably grow. Marketing assistance to enable independent producers to attend trade fairs, either through local subsidy or through Department of Trade and Industry funds, is important. The use of video in local companies could also be promoted, though professionals in the industry want to see greater awareness of the costs of high quality video production;
- local agencies may wish to encourage a bid for BBC and ITV night time franchises, should the Government go ahead with its plans to reallocate them. However Granada TV has a major interest in the ITV night time network. A local lobby prior to the Government making a decision would undoubtedly be opposed by Granada. If the Government do decide to reallocate, then it may well be that Granada would support a local bid.

*Enhancing the Communications Capabilities of Local Industry and Commerce*

Cable, satellite and microwave distribution are essential to the future efficiency of local industry. Comparable cities in Europe, such as Amsterdam and Cologne are developing advanced communications infrastructures. In Cologne this is taking the form of a Media Park which is designed to serve both the media industry and the business and commercial sectors.

Knowledge of these developments seems to be underdeveloped in Greater Manchester. Knowledge of their benefits is also underdeveloped. We recommend that building a local knowledge base in advanced communications should be given urgent priority. Advanced communications will affect all sections of the cultural industries and the wider business community. Without a strategy and without an adequate knowledge-base, Greater Manchester will fall behind its continental rivals.

A Communications Forum, in the process of investigating current demand for telecommunications services and planning for their continued development can help promote and stimulate the development of these services throughout the cultural industries and in the wider economy.

**Background Information**

*Developing a Strategy*

A strategy for television development ought to take account of the benefits it can confer on the arts and cultural industries and on industry and commerce as a whole. We believe the strategy should be structured so that it:
*promotes* new distribution capabilities in the region
*employs* new distribution technologies to stimulate local television production
*promotes* the wider dissemination of local arts and culture
*engages* the interests of the wider business community
is *designed* as a "communications" strategy for the Manchester conurbation.

Such a complex strategy would be aiming at promoting medium term development. Its complexity suggests the need for a forum, made up of decision makers, to discuss the range of issues which medium term development inevitably raises. The Forum would need to be oriented towards promoting profitable industrial development. Its membership must encompass the 10 AGMA authorities but must also comprise people who have executive, decision making authority. We do not recommend this forum as a new "talking shop". It should be a body which can take Greater Manchester's communications infrastructure into the 21st century. It should also ensure that such an infrastructure is developed to the benefit of local cultural producers and other sectors of the local economy.

It is possible that the established local broadcasters, Granada and BBC North West, could play a role in such a Forum. However we would caution against over dependence on these organisations. The White Paper is controversial because one of its main aims is to reduce their influence. The Forum would have to face decisions which imply greater competition in local broadcasting. It may be inappropriate to involve the established broadcasters in this process. The Forum's tasks would include commissioning feasibility work, bringing commercial partners together, assisting the development of coherent business plans, and winning the confidence of investors. Its deliberations would need to be confidential. It would also ensure that the benefits of investment would be realised across the conurbation. The recommendations in this report are designed to attract interest from all of the 10 authorities. However the City of Manchester, as a centre of commercial activity will inevitably benefit most from the strategy because of its role as regional centre.

We have also taken into account the potential impact of recommendations on existing broadcasters, particularly on Granada Television. We are confident that none of our proposals would damage the interests of existing broadcasters, nor would the proposals be opposed on commercial broadcasting grounds. The key elements of a strategy will need to incorporate the developments in: programme acquisition and distribution; technological convergence; deregulation. Media strategies elsewhere in the UK, have tended to be influenced more by changes in the system of programme acquisition than changes in the other areas. That is, they have tended to concentrate on the promotion of small scale independent television production.

Such a policy would have been appropriate six years ago when Channel 4 was first launched. The structure of the independent production sector has now settled into a mould which will be hard to break. Independent production is dominated by London. The facility provision sector is also dominated by London companies. These companies have many years of experience in managing creative innovation. Creative innovation is an intangible concept but it is absolutely central to the success of the London broadcasting industry. London is now recognised as a centre of excellence perhaps without parallel in Europe.

This presents a problem for regional media strategies. There is still some room for expansion, regionally, based on regional ITV companies subcontracting work locally. But the ITV companies represent a very limited market. The narrow structure of the industry means that this limited expansion creates a situation in which small independents become dependent on the regional broadcasters. A strategy has to go beyond this market, create new distributions channels, and build alliances in the European arena. That is, a strategy for the independents has to break down the structure of dependence.

This report places far greater emphasis on programme distribution, technological convergence and deregulation, than is normal in regional media strategies. We believe that a strategy to promote small scale independent production will have minimal impact unless these other issues are addressed. A consequence of this emphasis is that the reader will have to deal with some technical terminology with which he/she might be unfamiliar. This unfamiliarity, the very lack of a local knowledge base in new technologies is a major barrier to local economic development.

### *The Potential Impact of Deregulation and Technological Change Within the Industry*

A range of new technologies now available allow unprecedented expansion of the broadcast industry. The Government issued a Broadcasting White Paper in November 1988 partly to set the context for the expansion of broadcast and cable TV services. However there are market forces at work, over and above those identified in the White Paper, which also set the agenda for the development of this industry. The major factors influencing development in the coming five to ten years are:

- The expansion of broadcasting through a new channel (Channel 5).
- The separation of the two main functions in television - the production of programmes and the distribution of programmes.
- The enlarging of cable franchise areas from 100,000 homes to approx 500,000 homes, and the combination of Cable and Microwave distribution to speed up

the cabling process.
- An unprecedented growth in satellite communications facilities.
- The deregulation of telecommunications.

The White Paper on Broadcasting will be influential in determining the pace and direction of development only of the first three of these. Points four and five will be determined by wider developments in Europe and the United States. Before going onto consider this wider context, it is necessary first of all to explain the White Paper proposals in more detail.

*The Expansion of Broadcasting*

The major bottleneck preventing the development of a broader range of television and television related production, is the restriction on the distribution of TV programmes. Satellite communications have allowed entrepreneurs to expand the distribution system, ahead of Government plans to deregulate the television industry. However as yet, the take up of satellite receivers is unimpressive. Partly as a response to entrepreneurial activity the Government now proposes the following means of expanding TV distribution:
- A new channel, Channel 5, to being operations in 1993.
- Allocation on the two remaining channels on the British Satellite Broadcasting Direct Broadcast Satellite. This is expected to happen later this year.
- The introduction of local television services from 1991 onwards. These service would provide a combination of cable and microwave distribution systems.
- Microwave distribution systems exist at present in the United States.

The White Paper suggests no restriction on how local TV services might mix cable and microwave. It is conceivable, for example, that a system could be proposed which consisted entirely of microwave distribution. In an area such as Greater Manchester, one or two microwave transmitters would provide coverage of the whole conurbation at very low cost (approx £250,000 for a transmitter and installation). Such as system would provide possibly eight channels of television. The proposals ought to give considerable impetus to local television. However the Cable industry seems unenthusiastic.

*Separation of Production and Distribution*

The White Paper notes that the cost of entering the television industry deters new entrepreneurs and reduces the overall level of entrepreneurial activity. One of the main reasons for this is that commercially separate functions have been allocated, under licence, to the same companies. The industry has therefore been, until recently, quite monolithic.

The two major functions are production and distribution. The television industry began with the BBC, and later commercial franchisees, producing and distributing their own programmes. Such a system permitted few outsiders to gain a foothold in the industry. The Government has already gone some of the way towards segregating these functions. Channel 4 is a commissioning and distributing body but not a producer of its own programmes.The Government has asked the BBC and ITV companies to subcontract 25% of the production work for their schedules to independent producers.

The White Paper suggests a number of additional ways in which the major functions can be separated, with the ultimate objective of allowing greater entrepreneurial access at a lower entry cost. These include reallocation of the night time hours of one BBC channel by competitive tender, probably to a bidder which adopts the "commissioning" model, rather than the integrated functions model. Allocating Channel 5 in separate time blocks - i.e. separate franchises for different times of the day and night. Allocating a separate night hours franchise for the ITV network. It seems likely also that the successful Channel 5 tender will follow the "commissioning" model. The White Paper suggests one quite radical way of furthering the distinction between production and distribution. It is proposed that the transmission network currently run by the BBC and IBA will be privatised. The privatisation process will break the transmission network down into regions. Private companies will then be asked to tender to run regional transmission services. It is not clear, yet, how the new arrangements might work and what their impact might be.

*Enlarging the Cable Franchise Areas*

Over the past year the Cable Authority has begun to issue franchises for areas far larger than those envisaged by the Cable Authority Act 1984. In previous years Cable franchises tended to cover in the region of 100,000 homes. However one of the latest franchises covers 450,000 homes (Birmingham and Solihull). This trend ought to stimulate renewed interest in cable TV and cable services. This issue has become more important for the Greater Manchester area with the announcement by the Cable Authority in October, 1989 requesting tenders for five new franchise areas in the region, potentially reaching almost 850,000 homes.

The White Paper says that cable franchise holders will in future be allowed to extend their coverage by using microwave distribution systems. This ought to allow franchise holders to develop their subscriber base well in advance of cable networks being constructed. In other words cable companies will be able to develop a revenue base as they are committing resources to constructing the cable network. However there is ambiguity in these proposals. The Government envisages some form of local television but does not make clear how closely allied this will be to the cable industry. The Government proposes no restrictions on the use of microwave. This in turn opens up the possibility of separate cable and microwave systems in the same area. The Government also propose that Cable franchise holders cease to be the providers of services. The White Paper makes a tentative proposal that they become "common carriers". That is they provide the infrastructure for the delivery of services but do not actually provide services of their own.

*The Growth of Satellite Communications*

The satellite communications industry is too complex to summarise simply here. However, developments over the coming five years will have an impact on the television industry and on most sectors of industry in which rapid communications plays a significant role. The satellite industry as it affects the UK, is organised around two monopoly organisations - Intelsat, the

International Telecommunications Satellite Organisation; and Eutelsat, the European Telecommunications Satellite Organisation. These two organisations consist of the Post and Telecommunications Authorities of their signatory members in the case of the UK, British Telecom is the signatory.

The Post and Telecommunications Authorities, through Intelsat and Eutelsat, have a monopoly over the sale of satellite time. They also have a second monopoly, provided by domestic legislation. This is a monopoly over the right to "up-link" signals from earth stations to satellites. This dual monopoly, like all monopolies, inflates the cost of using satellites. However the monopoly is beginning to break down. Three major factors are at work: developments in European satellite communications; developments in U.S. satellite communications; deregulation of telecommunications.

*European Developments:* In Europe the launch of the ASTRA (1A) 16 channel medium powered satellite, in December 1988, was the first breach of Eutelsat's monopoly. ASTRA now plan to launch a second satellite ASTRA (1B). Like ASTRA (1A) this second satellite will carry 16 television channels. Partly in response to ASTRA, Eutelsat plans to launch 5 new 16 transponder () satellites in 1991/2. The overall impact of these developments is that between 1989 and 1992, European satellite capacity will have increased from 40 available transponders to 132 (excluding a reserve satellite operated by French Telecoms).

*Developments in the USA:* In the United States the Federal Communications Commission recently granted licenses to 8 private satellite operators to launch and operate their own satellite systems. At this stage it is impossible to gauge the likely impact of U.S. deregulation on satellite communications in Europe. It is possible to say however that American satellite operators will see Europe as a natural extension of their markets. The net effect of these trends in Europe and the U.S.A. will be an unprecedented growth in satellite activity.

*Deregulation in Telecommunications:* An additional factor adding to the exciting potential of satellite communications is the long term deregulation of telecommunications in the UK. Until recently the ability to "up-link" signals to satellites was the prerogative of British Telecom and Mercury Communications. In October 1988 the Department of Trade and Industry granted six additional "up-link" licenses. These licenses restrict the companies to distributing signals within the UK. However it is unlikely that this restriction will last beyond 1990/91. This means that by 1991 there will be greatly expanded satellite capacity and a far wider choice of companies which "up-link" signals. The overall impact should be a dramatic reduction in the costs of satellite communications.

### *The Impact of these Developments on the Local Economy*

Developments within the television industry, that is within the conventional structures, are unlikely to have an impressive impact on the rest of the local economy outside of broadcasting. The more dramatic and wider impact will emerge out of developments within satellite communications, and the combined use of cable and microwave distribution as a means of promoting local activity in the audio-visual industry.

It is difficult to be precise about this impact. It would take a far more detailed analysis of both the television industry and the demand for satellite communications to be precise about the benefits of developments in either. All we can offer here are a few impressionistic comments. However we do suggest that G.M.E.D. investigates further the likely up take of satellite communications and ways in which North West enterprises might take a dynamic role in this growing industry. It is perhaps best to look at the impact of the local economy under three headings: developments in conventional broadcasting; developments in cable TV; developments in satellite communications.

*Developments in Conventional Broadcasting*

The major changes here will be: allocation of a fifth channel, probably segregated into different time blocks; reallocation of BBC or ITV night time hours; the move towards subcontracting of programme production.

*Channel 5:* It is possible to estimate the impact of a fifth channel by reflecting on the impact of Channel 4, on the independent production sector. Although independent production companies existed prior to Channel 4, there is no doubt that Channel 4 has created this sector as it exists today. The impact of Channel 5 however is likely to be less impressive. First of all, it is not expected to reach more than 70% of the population. Much of the affluent South East will be outside of Channel 5's scope - undoubtedly reducing its earning potential. Finally the Channel will be divided into 2 or more time segments. A likely outcome for Channel 5 is that three segments will be allocated and that these will be distributed to organisations in different cities. A Manchester based organisation might be successful in applying for one of these segments.

The funding agencies might wish to support an organisation in a bid for a franchise. However they should be cautioned against undue optimism. The bid might be unsuccessful, and even if successful the Channel will face the following problems: integrating two or more services on one channel; low revenues because of the exclusion of areas of the South East, beginning in 1993 when satellite television will have been established for over 4 years, therefore presenting unprecedented levels of competition.

*The Night Time Franchises:* A more promising area of investment might be to encourage bids for the night hours on BBC or ITV. Night time viewing is already established, and the returns on investment can be evaluated properly.

*The 25% Subcontracting Rule:* The market for independent production is still expanding, though slowly by the standards of the early 1980's. The BBC and ITV companies are under an obligation to subcontract 25% of their programme output to smaller independent producers. There is scope here to strengthen the local independent production sector. Some investment in management training and skills training is necessary.

*Developments in Cable TV*

Three factors make Cable TV a more attractive proposition than at any time since the 1984 Cable Authority Act: the enlarging of franchise areas; the possibility of microwave distribution; inward investment from American cable interests. Two American companies are investing heavily in UK cable projects. A fourth factor is the C.E.C. RACE project which has resources to fund cable applications projects, where this is deemed to contribute to local economic regeneration.

Cable television is not a big provider of employment in the media. City Centre Cable's franchise for Westminster in London employs only 100 people. However the larger franchises are expected to create jobs for about 400 people. Skill requirements vary from the technical, to the administrative, to sales and marketing. Perhaps as important as the job creation issue, cable networks offer the possibility of new business services, as well as additional TV services.

These new business services tend to be underdeveloped in the UK. In Holland there is now a concerted effort being made to ensure that cable networks are exploited for a range of information services. Some of these could be particularly important for the development of Manchester's tourism industry. For example a local area database could be established providing:

- restaurant details including sample menus
- live venue details
- sites of interest
- local travel information
- automatic booking and ticket reservation.

Such a project could be developed in tandem with business services such as:

- database provision from the universities
- distance working
- a new local telephone network
- a computerised yellow pages.

Some domestic services, deliverable by cable, never seem to have caught the public's imagination. Nevertheless the technical possibility exists for:

- home banking
- home shopping
- and for new consumer teletext magazines.

Experiments are currently taking place along these lines in Amsterdam.

Manchester City centre and its environs would appear, on the face of things to provide the most suitable location for a cable TV network. It is possible however to conceive of a scheme which would link the city centre to the other Greater Manchester boroughs. The key issues to address are the forms of technology which a cable network would use, and the design of the network. In brief the options are: the appropriate mix of coaxial and fibre optic cable; a tree and branch or switched star configuration; the addition of microwave distribution. The most desirable long term solution is a sophisticated interactive system. Not only is the cost of such a system prohibitive. It is also unnecessary. There are a number of "hybrid" options, including the one adopted by the Dutch.

The Dutch system uses what is called a ministar, switching system. This links a group of homes by coaxial cable to an intermediate switching point. The switching point can then be linked either by fibre optic or coaxial cable to the cable headend. The system is also connected to the telephone network. Interactivity is achieved by way of signals passed down the telephone line to the system's information database. Information is then delivered via the cable system. This is a relatively low cost form of interactivity.

It is in the broad area of experimental new business and domestic services that G.M.E.D. might best justify stimulating interest in cable in Manchester. However it is clear that a number of issues need resolving before making a commitment to invest. An investigation of these issues normally forms the basis of a cable franchise application.

*Developments in Satellite Communications*

Satellite communications facilities serve both the media industry and the wider business community. Eutelsat's second generation of satellites, and developments in the USA suggest an unprecedented expansion in the use of satellite communications by business. However satellite facilities rely very heavily on media industries for their income. Business and media use are inseparable parts of the overall demand for satellite communications. The European Community is spending heavily on pilot applications projects which link satellite communications and local area fibre optic networks for business use. In Satcoms, therefore three distinct elements are coming together - fibre optic cable, satellite distribution for business use, and strategic planning for media development.

For the North West to play a significant role in the satellite era it needs to develop a strategy which links all three of these. Such a strategy is beyond the scope of this paper. However it is worth pointing out that other European cities are developing such strategies. In the Federal Republic of Germany, Cologne represents a state-of-the-art media and communications strategy. Hanover recently commissioned a strategy development paper which was delivered in February 1989. Kaarlsruhe is engaged in economic renewal based around advanced communications. In France Roubaix, and Ile de France, are similarly engaged in this form of strategy development. Barcelona in Spain, the Grand Duchy of Luxembourg, Amsterdam and Rotterdam in the Netherlands, are all looking to explore advanced communications systems as a means of attaining a competitive economic position in the 1990's. In London, Mercury Communications fibre-optic local network provides businesses with access, via the Thameside Teleport, to digital services to Europe and North America. Docklands customers also have access to:

- electronic mail
- financial information services
- Value Added Network Services in travel, health, insurance and retail
- voice messaging
- national paging
- high speed fax
- colour fax.

A Media strategy has to broaden out and take account of these business services, if the potential convergence of media and telecommunications technology is to be fully realised.

*Developments Elsewhere*

Reference has already been made to the development of a wider, advanced communications environment in London. In this section we look briefly at developments in the media field in different regions of the UK.

*London* is now a world centre of excellence in media production and distribution. It is impossible to estimate the size of the television production industry in London. Apart from the presence of two major ITV franchise holders (Thames and London Weekend) London is also host to Independent Television News, which produces news programmes for ITV, Channel 4, BSB, and until recently for SuperChannel. All the major ITV franchise holders have a London base. SKY Television's 5 channel service is based in West London. British Satellite Broadcasting's headquarters is in London. The BBC's major production and administration headquarters are in London. About 15 satellite channels operate out of London, including one Scandinavian and until recently one Spanish channel.

Channel 4 is based in London, and most of the independent producers who make programmes for Channel 4 are also based there. One comparative statistic is worth noting. The Independent Programme Producers Association is a body set up to represent independent producers after the founding of channel 4. The main qualification of its members is that they are "in production", i.e. actively making TV programmes. The IPPA has around 600 members. Of these we counted 437 companies which are London based. We counted only 9 based in Manchester (the second media city). London is also the home of the UK's production facilities industry, and a recognised centre of excellence in TV computer graphics.

All these factors give London an unassailable lead in the TV industry. This lead is technical (i.e. they have the best resources in production facilities), and it is creative (i.e. TV professionals have a wide scope of facilities on which to experiment and create new visual forms). It has also a lead in distribution technology. The regions can only hope to snipe at this commanding lead.

*Birmingham* now has a designated Media development zone, in Digbeth, and a Media Development Agency created by the City Council. The City's Media Strategy is based on a document produced by Comedia Consultants. The strategy calls for the appointment of a Media Development director to head up a Media development Agency which would:
- promote and the market the media sector
- provide information, consultancy, and assistance on financial resources
- co-ordinate media training
- improve distribution networks locally
- participate in trade fairs, conferences and exhibitions
- create a directory of media resources in Birmingham
- initiate new media businesses.

There will also be a Media enterprise centre providing space for 60 - 70 business, and providing common facilities and services However the Media Development Agencies budget is small - £150,000 for the first year. The post of Director was advertised recently at £18,000. This in a high earning industry is too low to attract a Director with sufficient industry experience. The budget is also wildly underestimated. The strategy takes little account of new distribution technologies and is, in our view, short sighted.

The more interesting developments in Birmingham are private sector led. Birmingham is expected to be the location of 3 of the new private satellite service providers. It may also be chosen as the site of British Aerospace's control facilities for their new Orion satellite venture. The largest cable franchise in the UK was recently granted to a Birmingham consortium with a potential reach of 450,000 homes. In cable and satellite, Birmingham looks set to achieve an impressive new infrastructure. Greater Manchester ought to look more closely at these developments and consider its own competitive position vis-a-vis the Midlands.

*Newcastle and the North East:* the development of media activity in the North Eat is co-ordinated by the North East Media Development Agency, based in Newcastle-upon-Tyne. The emphasis in the North Eat is on participatory workshops. The workshop movement began as an experiment funded by Channel 4, supported by the industry, with the aim of encouraging new talent in the community, to make television programmes about the community. The North East has been very successful at harnessing this model. There are now about 60 people employed in workshops. NEMDB has a Media Training centre based in Gateshead. The facility consists of studio space, professional camera equipment (video and film); lower grade recording equipment; editing facilities and a viewing theatre. It offers a 2 year film and video production course and it offers a range of short course to interested individuals and organisations.

*Bristol*'s Watershed was one of the first media centres in the UK. The project began in the late 1970's and has received funding and support from: the British FIlm Institute, Sun Life Assurance, Kodak, ICI Paints and Fibres, and British Telecom. The centre provides media training, a viewing theatre, and photography exhibition space.

*A Review of the Wider Geographical Context, Particularly of Developments in Europe*

As in all areas of the media industry it is necessary to consider European developments in both production and distribution. We have already made reference to the trend towards co-producing TV programmes. This allows production costs to be shared and it opens up second country sales. It is essential for Manchester based independent producers to participate in this trend, and to have access to European co-production finance. The Commission of the European Community is sponsoring an 11 point programme aimed at stimulating production skills and capacity, and distribution channels, in Europe. The C.E.C. also has projects to develop distance learning by broadcast media. National and regional policy makers in Europe are turning to the communications media as vehicles for the regeneration of their economies. This section looks at the two most important European developments. The MEDIA and related C.E.C. programmes, and regional media policy.

*The C.E.C. (Commission for the European Communities):* Commercial television in Europe does not have the same strong tradition that it has in the UK. The Scandinavian countries, the Netherlands, and Belgium have all resisted private commercial TV until recently. The Scandinavian's are now reluctantly adopting some form of commercial TV (in Norway this is simply a case of allowing commercial TV on local cable stations). The Belgians launched their first private commercial station earlier this year. In the Netherlands the very strong print publishing tradition has so far managed to ward off private commercial television. Overall however the picture is of expansion, including new commercial channels in countries which previously had none, and more commercial channels in countries such as France, the UK (Channel 4 and soon Channel 5), and Germany. Added to this are approx 30 cross frontier services.

This expansion has been met, to an alarming degree, by programme imports from the USA. In order to combat this, and to strengthen the European TV industry the C.E.C. has considered introducing European production quotas. These are unlikely to be enforced, but in fact do not need to be as most countries have domestic quotas. The C.E.C. has set up a number of programmes in an attempt to assist the wider communications industry which include the MEDIA, RACE, DELTA, COMETT and shortly, DEUCE. All of these are pertinent to the industry to varying degrees. Further details are available in the interim report.

*Regional Policy Initiatives:* This report has already made mention of the ways in which some regions of Europe are planning to exploit the convergence of different communications technologies. These projects combine media, telecoms, and computer based technology. The best developed example of this is Cologne.

The Cologne Media Park is both a Media Park and a Teleport. In this context a Teleport should be understood as a clearing house for international communications. The Park is a fifty acre site on a former railway station and goods yard. It is excepted that six satellite television services will operate out of there. This level of satellite use is a sufficient base upon which to build a wider telecommunications service for business users. The concept is being used to attract design, graphic design and studio facilities to the area. Of the various television services, it is likely that three will involve a measure of inward investment from: Canal Plus, a French Pay TV service looking to extend its interests abroad; CLT, of Luxembourg which runs the German language RTL Plus service; Fininvest, of Italy, which also has interests in France

*Hanover:* The City of Hanover recently received a 150 page report outlining in detail the major trends in the media, telecommunications and computer industries. The report focuses on the inevitable convergence of the technological base of these industries and it outlines medium term plans to capitalise on them. The planning model includes:

- projected developments in the audio-visual industry;
- projected developments in the print medium;
- the convergence of media, telecoms and computer industries;
- a strategy for the educational sector to provide co-ordinated;
- instruction in these technologies;

- a strategy for the development of the design function in the media industries;
- the development of software and image libraries;
- film development;
- developments in advanced television systems such as 3-D TV, and High Definition TV;
- developments in interactive video and interactive discs.

This is an impressive catalogue of developments in the coming five years and if adopted as a media strategy should put Hanover a the leading edge of the communications industries.

*Luxembourg* has a population of around 300,000, smaller than the City of Manchester and less than an eighth of the population of Greater Manchester. Despite its small size Luxembourg is one of the major players in the television export market. The 16 channel ASTRA (1B) satellite was an initiative of the Luxembourg Government. It eventually found acceptance and funding from various investors around Europe. CLT, the Compagnie Luxembourg de T l fusion, has interests in French Television and German Television. Luxembourg is now considering plans to turn Luxembourg city into a centre of media excellence for Europe.

*The Netherlands* was one of the first European countries to develop a near national cable network. The Dutch Government is now sponsoring pilot projects aimed at developing information services for use within the cable network. This is a prelude to upgrading the network to more widespread use of fibre optics. One of the pilot project areas is Amsterdam, where a city-wide information service is being developed. This will provide information on all cultural activities in the City and an automatic booking and billing service. The Amsterdam experiment will also provide electronic yellow pages and a range of comparable information services. The projects are overtly experimental, aiming to test the likely uptake of information provision through cable.

Greater Manchester could learn a great deal from these experiments, both about the potential demand for information services delivered by cable, and about low cost interactive technology.

**Conclusion**

In the preceding sections, this report has looked at a variety of developments across the broadcast and communications industries. In this section the most significant developments are brought together, to suggest a coherent strategy for media development in the coming five years.

The types of projects identified, and our research amongst broadcast professionals suggest it will be difficult to extend the benefits of a strategy to the 10 AGMA authorities. The core Manchester area (the City centre, Salford, Trafford Park) is overwhelmingly the most attractive place in which to invest. Elsewhere entrepreneurial activity is low. Even in Manchester, the level of entrepreneurial activity appears to us to be low in comparison with, for example, Cardiff and Glasgow. The distinction made in this report, between production and distribution, seems to us critical in this respect. If the benefits of a strategy are to be felt beyond the core area, then GMED must look closely at investing in, or encouraging investment in, new forms of distribution.

We are not convinced that policies adopted in other parts of the UK should act as a model for Greater Manchester. The development of TV workshops and subsidised training facilities, as for example in the North East, did not seem to interest out interviewees. The use of Council backed facilities in Sheffield has been successful because of the low level of activity there. Birmingham's Media Strategy, based on a new Media centre, appears already to be running into trouble. Private sector initiatives in Birmingham, especially in cable and satellite, seem to hold out more for the future than do public sector initiatives there, simply because these are new distribution technologies which local policy can help shape to local needs.

In Greater Manchester the media business is staunchly independent. Although there are clear gaps in training provision the priority should be to provide the industry with access to new markets. This brings us back to new distribution technologies, and points to a need for European links. We are also of the view that, if the funding agencies help promote new distribution technologies, then the new links between media production and local arts and culture can be used for mutual benefit. For example a cable franchise can provide an outlet for local artistic production, as well as help promote it, through a local arts information service. Satellite TV can provide a vehicle for local live events, and local artistic excellence. That in turn implies a boost to local media production. New distribution technologies offer the best opportunity for development across the range of arts and cultural industries and they also offer scope for improving the efficiency of the local business and commercial community. As such investment in these distribution technologies provides an opportunity for public/private sector cooperation which could benefit both the culture industry and the wider business community in the region.

# 4 The popular music industry

*Steve Redhead*

**Introduction**

There are always difficulties in defining activities which would come under the heading of "popular culture", but for the purposes of this particular study this term has been taken to encompass the popular music industry. This report refers specifically to work done on the popular music industry in Greater Manchester. Special attention has been paid to size, structure, differentiation within the industry, and the potential for development in the Greater Manchester area. Here we concentrate on mapping the current state of the local industry and developing a strategy for increasing production and distribution in this sector of the local cultural industries.

Greater Manchester is a region with an international reputation for popular music production by independent record companies. Factory Records - and its related projects like the Hacienda and Dry - has dominated the area for the last decade and become the role model for other independent companies to follow, both inside and outside the locality.

However, the sales of "independent" records have declined considerably since their high point in the aftermath of punk in the late 1970s. Independent record companies wishing to copy Factory's success today are faced with a likely sales figure for their product which is only a fraction of what could have been achieved ten years ago with similar reviews, publicity and marketing. The local record companies in the popular music industry consequently comprise tiny, often transient, businesses which exist to market the product of one or two bands or singers. This is not necessarily a drawback, since the dynamism of the industry world-wide has historically stemmed precisely from the short-term entrepreneurial initiatives of small independent companies.

The absence of major record companies from the region has meant that local independent businesses have regularly played the role of A and R (Artists and Repertoire) personnel usually employed by the bigger record companies to spot, and sign, talent. The predictable outcome has frequently been the loss of the performers to major labels, usually based in London. In many cases no formal legal contract exists between the small independent company and the artists ; as a consequence no financial reward accrues to the local industry once the artists in question have signed to another label.

The manufacture, design and distribution of the local industry's product is, however, mainly carried on by companies outside the region, usually in the South East, or even in other European countries such as France. Greater Manchester is known for its large pool of artists, venues and recording facilities not its manufacture, design and distribution of the related commodities (videos, t-shirts, records, tapes etc) themselves. However an important infrastructure of record "pluggers", promotions companies, lawyers, accountants, music publishers and others exists already in the Greater Manchester area.

There are three major dimensions of the popular music industry: production, distribution and consumption. This report is concerned with proposals on strategy for expansion which largely relate to the first two; production, and distribution. The industry consists of a whole number of organisations and personnel. The main ones are :

- Pressing Plants
- Recording Studios/Engineers/Producers
- Musicians/Singers
- Disc Jockeys
- Video Producers
- Music Publishers
- Musicians Union
- Music Press
- Radio
- Record Shops
- Promoters
- Record Companies.

Record companies can be divided into major and independent, or "indie". However, though the transnational majors such as Sony/CBS, WEA are distinct from the independents, the independents themselves can be further subdivided. Noreena Ann Davies, (Harvester Press, 1987), argues that there are four groups of record companies, namely : the majors; the major independents; the independents; small individual companies. The majors are distinct from the others because of their scale and the fact that the following tasks are usually performed within the organisation; distribution, A and R, production, marketing, publicity, promotion, publicity, international aspects.

The trend in recent years has been for the majors to become part of worldwide media conglomerates; Sony's takeover of CBS is a classic example. Major independents, meanwhile, have struggled to survive takeover by the majors. The best known recent example is the surprise takeover, by a major, of

Chris Blackwell's Island label, one of the most famous, respected and commercially successful "major independents". The independents and small individual companies have correspondingly felt the effect of the "globalisation" of the popular music industry in the 1980s as new markets were exploited e.g. Africa, China and the industry reorganised. Such reorganisation has been prompted by: profitability crises in the music business of the late 1970s and early 1980s; demographic changes i.e.the drop in numbers of young people under 25; new technologies such as video, tape to tape cassette recorders, compact discs and digital audio cassette (DAT).

Such distinctions between types of record companies as made by Noreena Ann Davies are always difficult to maintain, especially if the "independent" record company retains a licensing agreement with a major. Notwithstanding such problems, the categories can be usefully applied to the record companies operating in the Greater Manchester area. There are no major record companies situated in the Greater Manchester district.

Factory Records, with its pop video offshoot IKON and connected projects like the Hacienda (club) and Dry (bar) is a particularly pertinent example of a successful Major Independent. Granada television presenter, Anthony Wilson, has been the main figure behind such developments. Named after Andy Warhol's Factory in New York, Wilson's record label has in and since the punk era made a significant impression in the international popular music industry for more than a decade. Created as a "design centre", all of its products are carefully conceived as having a recognisable identity. In the early days design students from Manchester Polytechnic, such as Peter Saville, formed an important part of Factory Communications' commitment to a particular marketable image. The opening at the beginning of the decade of the Hacienda (part owned by New Order, formerly Joy Division, and Factory Records' most high profile signing), a distinctively designed night club, marked an even more remarkable stage in the place of the company, and personnel's, role in the local music industry. It has over the last seven years become one of the leading nightclubs and live venues in the United Kingdom. The opening of the bar, Dry, in 1989 and the planned transformation of a former warehouse on Princess Street into the new centre for the company, suggests a revamping of the Factory product for the 1990s. Such a revamping was further emphasised with the development of avant garde/classical music production, which we understand received support from The Arts Council.

On the other hand, Play Hard Records, run by Dave Haslam and Nathan McGough, is a young, expanding independent record company. Play Hard grew out of the magazine Debris, written and produced by Haslam, who, has also played a key role in the local popular music industry as a Disc Jockey at clubs such as the Hacienda and Isadoras. Play Hard was formed to put out a various artists LP release "Head Over Ears" with a special issue of Debris magazine in 1987. The label has subsequently been described in the music press as "one of Britain's leading independents" with a roster of artists including MC Buzz B, The Train Set, The Bodines and King of the Slums. Nathan McGough is also manager of one of the region's best supported Factory bands, Happy Mondays.

Most of the rest of the independent record labels in the area come into the category of small individual companies. They rise, and fall and disappear, with considerable rapidity. In certain cases labels have been formed solely to promote the product of the band itself ; Cow is, for example, the label formed by Inspiral Carpets.

However, special mention should be made of Bop Cassettes, a voluntary association established to promote "minority" music and arts, with support funding from North West Arts. Bop Cassettes began as, uniquely, a tape cassette only label, though it has ventured into vinyl recording more recently. A move into premises at New Mount Street will give it a more city based image and consolidate its "consultancy" role for North West Arts. Since 1987 Bop Cassettes has disseminated its knowledge about applying for North West Arts grants to numerous bands and individuals wishing to start labels within the popular music industry in Greater Manchester, playing a vital educational role in the process. An expansion of such a role might be one possible future trajectory for Bop Cassettes.

Recording studios like Out of The Blue and Suite 16 have gained a certain reputation both inside and outside the region, but it is Strawberry Studios which is most often linked to Greater Manchester in the pop consumer's mind because of the group 10cc, amongst others such as Barclay James Harvest, recording there in the 1970s. Performers wishing to attract the attention of record companies usually first make a "demo" tape. Recording studios are available in Greater Manchester at various rates for bands wishing to book studio time. The same applies once record companies have "signed" them up and want them to make a record. Various studios are used depending on the sort of sound the company and performers want. Rehearsal rooms, too, are available, but the importance of the much-used instrument shops in the region as meeting places and ad hoc rehearsal spaces should not be underestimated.

Manufacturing the record from the master tape has traditionally been done outside the region. Cutting the master tape onto lacquer and the subsequent pressing of the required number of vinyl records, and label and sleeve design services, have been done by various different contractors (n.b. the use of digital audio cassette, or DAT, is beginning to make such a procedure much easier, quicker and cheaper, obviating the need for a master tape). Invariably London cutting services have been used, and pressing subcontracted by those companies, frequently to France and other European countries. However, these services have become available inside the region with the setting up of the small cutting and pressing company, Hot Knife, in October 1988.

Nationwide publicity in the music press and media has established Manchester firmly as a popular music centre. The area shared in the British "beat" boom of the 1960s featuring such bands as Herman's Hermits, The Hollies and Wayne Fontana and the Mindbenders. In the later 1970s it was a centre for punk and new wave bands and venues. In the 1980s The Smiths, in particular, gained massive, world wide publicity for the region. At a recent Smiths convention - which took place after the band had broken up - at the University of Manchester over 900 people flocked to the city from many different countries. Additionally, the Contact Youth Theatre have recently performed Robert Graham's play about The Smiths, "If You Have Five Seconds To Spare", at Manchester University's Contact Theatre. It is still, though, the city's past involvement in the unleashing of hundreds of punk bands and dozens of independent labels in the mid-late 1970s that is often remembered. The G-Mex Centre hosted a well attended ten year celebration of Manchester's punk past in 1986, and the "post-industrial" look of the Hacienda is frequently cited as a continuation of a post-punk design tradition.

More recently the city's international reputation has been enhanced with its involvement in thriving "indie-pop" as well as house and hip-hop dance music scenes, Venues and clubs of all types continue to expand in the region. This is important especially with the rapid change in recent years whereby, in the formation of house and hip-hop music in particular, Disc Jockeys came to the forefront of the music industry. Instead of merely playing records on radio or in clubs, Disc Jockeys have increasingly become producers/makers of their own records. The traditional division of labour in the popular music industry is rapidly changing, enabling take up on a massive scale of the potential of new technologies. Two significant consequences follow from such changes: one is the use of domestic premises to record high quality material for record release. Home recording, and production, is no longer a problem. The other is the relative decline of the conventional notion of a concert or "gig". Clubs rather than venues consequently take on a greater role in the local nightime economy than hitherto, without, however, displacing the pre-eminent role of the "live" venue.

**Recommendations**

Our recommendations are geared to harnessing many different aspects of the music industry in a strategy which will enhance its role in the local economy in the 1990s and beyond.

*Multi-Purpose Venues*

A new, medium sized multi-purpose venue should be considered for the region. It might seek to do for the 1990s what the Hacienda did so successfully for Manchester in the 1980s. This could, in principle, be situated in the city centre or in, or around, any of the outlying towns of the Greater Manchester area. However a city centre venue would be useful given the relatively poor facilities currently existing for "medium-sized" bands ie. those that more than fill the International 1 but not the Apollo or Free Trade Hall. The kinds of "popular" music - and other arts - to be promoted should be wide ranging ie. including avant-garde/classical, jazz, dance etc. The venue should be designed so as to maximise the exploitation of the new telecommunication technologies e.g. satellite links with Europe. This recommendation should be considered closely with the question of the development of an entertainments quarter for the city, as indeed could all of the recommendations in this report.

An extra large multi-purpose venue should be considered. It is noteworthy that the Greater Manchester district has no satisfactory major venue for "super-bands" e.g. Prince, Bruce Springsteen, Simple Minds, Madonna. There is no local equivalent of Roundhay Park in Leeds, so professional soccer stadia like Maine Road have had to be utilised. Construction of a large new purpose-built "super" venue should be considered in relation to the city's Olympic bid for 1996 so that it could be pre-planned as a site where professional and amateur sports, as well as arts and entertainment on a large scale could be catered for.

New, smaller venues for the various districts (e.g. Oldham) in the Greater Manchester area should be discussed. These might take the form of conversions of current buildings to make them more suitable. We recommend that local authorities in the different areas consider the possibility of development on the lines of The Citadel venue in St Helens, a successful local authority venture.

These initiatives would, additionally, provide a focal point for showing investors and consumers alike that there is a viable and expanding popular music industry in the Greater Manchester area.

*Independent Record Distribution Network*

A new distribution company should be created for the region, and beyond. The scope and need for an appropriate distribution network for independent records in the region is clear. Whilst it would not necessarily have to rely solely on the product of the Greater Manchester area a trans-Pennine link might be worth considering, for instance - such a base would give a distinct advantage. Greater Manchester is certainly well equipped for any distribution activity, particularly with the advent of the European single market in 1992.

It may be worth looking at the possibility of linking such a distribution group with two other recommendations in this report; on cutting/pressing plants, and on retail outlets. We recommend that a new, locally based distribution network for independent records should be considered, possibly encompassing the North West, or even North, of England.

*Record, Tape and Compact Disc Manufacturing Facilities*

An expansion of existing facilities in the region for the manufacture of records, tape cassettes and compact discs should be urgently considered. This might take the form of investment in the small, independent production company already dealing with cutting and pressing  vinyl records and label and sleeve design. This however should be dependent on proper quality control being established There should also be extra investment in compact disc and vinyl production over and above this e.g. the funding of new manufacturing plant to be situated in the region to create competition.

*Retail Outlets*

New forms of retailing for the local popular music industry should be explored. This would involve two major aspects : new technologies e.g. adopting the practice of some stores in the USA of "mix & match" cassettes, where customers bring cassette tapes to the retailer who then records various tracks onto the tape at the customer's request; changes in the selling environment e.g. developing the social aspects of record shops as "meeting places" by establishing links with other related industries (clothes, shoes, hairdressing etc) and providing other services (coffee bars etc) on, or near, the premises. Both of these aspects might best be accomplished by the setting up of managed workspace, possibly within an entertainments quarter.

*Managed Workspace*

We believe that the local popular music industry needs to look for a wider co-ordination and sharing of services. The most likely solution to this problem would be the utilisation of a building, or buildings, in the Greater Manchester area for managed workspace. Rehearsal rooms might be situated there, but its most important function would be to offer accommodation for currently disparate small businesses operating in the Greater Manchester popular music industry offering a wide range of goods and services e.g. independent record labels, listings magazines, record cover and label design, pop video production, record promotions etc. A business advice service for bands and artists could also be incorporated, and the emphasis placed on training.

*Centre of Excellence*

Possibly as an extended aspect of the development of managed workspace, we recommend the creation of a "centre of excellence". This might also be connected to, or comprise part of, a Media Centre as recommended by Haydn Shaughnessy in his interim report on the Television Broadcasting Sector. There are a number of reasons why the closely related businesses of popular music and television should be given some kind of physical proximity in the Greater Manchester area. A Centre of Excellence should comprise top of the range recording studios, pop video production facilities and a design centre. There is no reason why the series of local studios could not be linked to a city based Centre of Excellence but a high quality studio in the midst of a whole array of other art-design related activities has a number of advantages. Not the least of these is profile. There is an urgent need for Greater Manchester's recording industry to capitalise on its reputation and to establish itself as a place where people, including those from other European countries, would want to come to record in the future.

*Popular Music Officer for North West Arts*

We recommend the consideration of a post of Popular Music Officer at North West Arts. This would in principle be a specialist post designed to ensure that popular music would not be marginalised within cultural policy for the arts as tends to be the case at present in Greater Manchester. A major role initially would be to co-ordinate the consideration, and if appropriate, implementation of recommendations in this report. A team of local participants would need to be identified and co-ordinated, including representatives of relevant development corporations, record companies, recording studios and local authorities. One role of such an officer at North West Arts might be to identify and help to disseminate "best practice" within this field. Furthermore, such a post would furnish the possibility of compiling and publishing a pop industry directory ie. names and addresses of companies and individuals connected to the popular music industry in Greater Manchester. This could function both as a publicity device and trade directory for potential customers.

**Background**

There are at present at least two other related studies which have recently been carried out which pertain to the popular music industry in the North West. One, less directly, is the COMEDIA study for Manchester City Council, GMED and others. The other is the University of Liverpool Institute of Popular Music study of the popular music industry on Merseyside for Liverpool City Council. In view of these related research developments which have implications for the North West music industry, CER feels that early consideration of this report is desirable. Both of these related studies were initially motivated by developments elsewhere, such as the Cultural Industries Quarter in Sheffield and The City Centre in Dublin.

The Cultural Industries Quarter in Sheffield, developed in conjunction with Sheffield City Council, now comprises a series of interlocking projects on sites close to each other and includes three projects of particular relevance to the pop music industry. First, Red Tape studios, run by Sheffield City Council, offering recording, rehearsal and training facilities to local musicians, especially the unemployed. Second, The Leadmill, which opened in 1982 as a music, dance and arts centre, and established itself as a live venue. Third, sound recording studios, involving the studios of local bands Comsat Angels and Human League, and local independent label FON.

These and other developments have been brought together to form the Audio Visual Enterprise Centre (AVEC) which involves development of recording studios and photographic gallery among other features, and is intended to provide sound and vision cable link direct to The Leadmill from each of the 24 track broadcast quality recording studios in the complex, providing the opportunity for direct telecommunications link to television studios. The City Centre in Dublin, part funded by the rock group U2 and Yamaha instruments, comprises cheap rehearsal rooms and graphic design studio as well as planned theatre rehearsal space and artists studios.

The general conclusion which CER reached after initial pilot research into the local popular music industry was that simply reproducing an AVEC or equivalent for the Greater Manchester region was not desirable. We were aware that COMEDIA were considering the possibility of establishing an AVEC type centre in their study for Manchester city council and GMED and others, and that the Institute of Popular Music at the University of Liverpool were studying both AVEC in Sheffield and the entire music scene in Liverpool for their report to Liverpool city council. Our interviews with personnel in Sheffield, however, confirmed our impression that the development of the respective local popular music economies was entirely different. However, a strategy for expansion of this sector of the Greater Manchester economy may well have to depend on related sorts of intervention, both public and private, despite Greater Manchester's advanced state within the national popular music industry.

AVEC, and other aspects of the Cultural Industries Quarter, clearly filled a requirement in the Sheffield region, once the bottom fell out of traditional heavy industry there. Cultural industries tended to replace traditional ones. The Manchester music scene has evolved alongside the region's traditional industries and developing service sector, over a much longer period, and has characteristically displayed an independent entrepreneurship unmatched outside London. More importantly the intertwined relationships of the participants in the music industry in Greater Manchester meant that there was not the same need for bringing people together as there was in Sheffield. On top of this, facilities such as recording studios abound in Manchester. Bands from Liverpool and Sheffield, for example, as well as elsewhere, have tended to record in Manchester.

Our conclusion was therefore that although the direct following of an AVEC model would not be appropriate for Greater Manchester there would have to be consideration of the feasibility of a focal point, or points, in the region which might play the kind of role AVEC and other features of the Cultural Industries Quarter have done in Sheffield ie. acting as a flagship, giving a high profile to intervention in the cultural industries, and heightening public perception of both daytime and nightime economies in the region.

To furnish CER with the information to conduct the study of the popular music sector a comprehensive list of participants in the production and distribution side of the industry in Greater Manchester has been compiled. This is the first time such an extensive survey has been conducted. The list used for sending out questionnaires for the "volume" part of the Arts and Cultural Industries project included :

- Independent Record Labels
- Recording Studios
- Record Producers
- Rehearsal Studios
- Record Production Companies
- Live Venues/Clubs
- Music Publishers
- Video Producers
- Record Cutting/Pressing Plant.

Interviews were conducted with samples of these participants, both face to face and by telephone. We feel that the information compiled as a result of this survey should be utilised so that a Greater Manchester Pop Directory is regularly produced. This would consist of names and addresses of companies and individuals linked to the popular music industry in the area. The purpose of this directory would be twofold. It could firstly act as a publicity device for giving a high public profile to the industry as a whole and to its individual components. Secondly, it could act as a trade directory for potential customers of the various services and facilities. As we make clear in our recommendations, production of such a directory could be part of the brief for the post of a newly created North West Arts Popular Music/Cultural Industries Officer.

Our recommendations follow from our analysis of the popular music industry in Greater Manchester as a kind of "sleeping giant". The imperative need in our view is investment at a series of points in the production and distribution process. However the industry suffers from business perception of it as not a "proper" industry. The recommendations are designed to overcome this perception and clarify the particular needs of the industry as it prepares for the changes to be brought about by the single European market in 1992 and the deregulation of the Television Broadcasting sector.

Below we present the rest of the findings of our study which form the basis of our recommendations. Our respondents have been generous with their time and we thank them for their co-operation.

*Venues*

Greater Manchester has a whole variety of venues for popular music. Some have established a national, and even international reputation. The Band on The Wall, for instance, has had strong past connections to hosting live jazz music which it still maintains whilst expanding its field to cover a variety of modern musics - reggae, latin, blues, country and folk. It has become an important trading arm and venue for Inner City Music, the organisation at the forefront of the city's contemporary jazz scene and new music developments.

The Apollo and Free Trade Hall are the city's main seated concert venues but neither were purpose built for the sorts of rock and pop audiences created by today's markets. Salford, and Manchester University Unions together with Manchester Polytechnic and UMIST confirm the importance of the huge student population as consumers of live popular music in the city. The fact that Manchester has the largest educational campus in Europe should remain a major factor in strategies for the expansion of the sector.

Clubs like the two Internationals and The Boardwalk have featured prominently in attracting both "home-based" talent and internationally known musicians and singers. Despite the preponderance of clubs and live venues, there are clearly not enough venues in the region which are geared to specific needs. There are hundreds of bands and performers in the Greater Manchester region alone, and a bottleneck in outlets for their performance. The identifiable gaps in provision on the basis of our interviews and observations are as follows.

Smaller venues outside the city centre. Not only are there bands queuing up to play - there are waiting lists for venues - but a development (ie.conversion or refurbishment) of such venues would help to capture the market which cannot afford to come into the city centre. One possibility which might be considered is the idea of local authority ventures on the lines of The Citadel, a local authority funded venue in St. Helens.

A new "medium-sized" venue in the city centre, geared to live performance. This could involve either a conversion (say a warehouse) or a purpose built building. Its design should aim to incorporate a wide variety of live popular music (from avant garde to pop) which is presently showcased at a range of unsuitable venues in the Greater Manchester area. It should have bar and fast food/restaurant facilities. It should also be geared to sound and vision links which would enable the recording of live events and provide more generally for telecommunications links to television studios including satellite and cable television. There are good precedents for this; Riverside Studios in Newcastle was used successfully for live broadcasting of Channel 4's early-mid 1980s pop show "The Tube", and more recently the successful BBC2 programme "East of Eden" consisted of concerts recorded at a live venue in Scotland. Manchester currently lacks exactly this type of venue. Private funding should be sought for such a venture.

A new "super" venue for "stadium" sized audiences. As Sheffield has linked much of its cultural development to the World Student Games to be held in the city in 1991, Manchester could profitably benefit from its bid to host the 1996 Olympic Games. There has already been preliminary consideration of a multi-purpose sports stadium in the North West. This discussion should be expanded to take in the creation of "stadium" sized facilities for live popular music in the 1990s and beyond. The Olympic Games bid has already created the linking of numerous cultural events (including youth/street/pop culture) over the coming year to the application for the city to be considered as a contender in 1996. The yoking together of plans for a stadium with sport and popular entertainment in mind would be a natural outcome of this process.

*Distribution*

The distribution of major record company product is all organised from outside the region. As far as independent record distribution is concerned the network is in a state of flux. Rough Trade, then only a music shop in London, set up its independent distribution network, The Cartel, some years ago, creating an important new way to get records into the shops other than via the majors. Different independent companies were responsible for different parts of the British independent markets, divided by region.

As far as the North West was concerned Probe Plus, a record shop and independent label on Merseyside, performed a distribution function for a time. This arrangement proved to be inefficient - though it is still functioning - and gradually Red Rhino, a York record shop and responsible for the Northern region for The Cartel took over distribution of independent records in the North West.

However, financial problems caused Red Rhino to go into liquidation in autumn 1988. Since then the vacuum left by the demise of Red Rhino has been filled by Nine Mile and APT. Nine Mile is the Midlands representative of The Cartel. APT, which has replaced Red Rhino in York but is based in other European countries, is effectively the British arm of Belgian independent record company Play It Again Sam. It has managed to include the price of record manufacture in its distribution costs, and has so far managed to operate more cheaply than British firms despite carriage charge. The problem with APT is that Red Rhino's creditors resent the emergence of a "new" company in place of the old without their own debts being settled.

There is clear evidence from our research that a fresh distribution system (possibly using existing companies on a co-operative basis, or else creating an entirely new organisation) based in Manchester covering the North of England should be inaugurated. There are current precedents for independent distribution networks outside The Cartel e.g. Southern Studios' distribution of independent records throughout the country including Greater Manchester.

We believe that Greater Manchester is the only region in the country which can compete with London. It has excellent road and rail communication, plus first class airport facilities. A new distribution network would help not just to attract and keep local bands in the North but would start to expand the exploitation of the European wide market. Increasingly the European market is becoming a rival with the USA for the types of independent music produced in the region. If seen in the context of chapter three of this report, on the Television Broadcasting sector, linking up European "pop" markets through satelliite etc, a new distribution network should not just be concentrating on the small British market in future. It should also consider the possible exploitation of new technologies such as video, DAT and compact disc which have not been as prevalent in the independent sector as in the majors.

*Manufacture*

At present no compact disc manufacturing facilities are available in the region; only one company is manufacturing in the North West as a whole. Hot Knife, a post production cutting and pressing plant for vinyl records, has begun, on a small scale, to fill the gap in manufacture in the region up to 1988. The company expected to cater for a demand that they were sure existed. They are now starting to create a demand among local independent companies. Local bands who had not considered getting their demo tapes onto vinyl before are beginning to use the service, with or without record company help. In the past such bands had got to the stage of having a master tape of their material but had found it daunting and difficult to deal with various companies in London. Hot Knife have discovered that bands often lacked the knowledge of the advantages of a cutting studio in the region. Though they had been willing to pay money for sleeve design and general art work, they had not been prepared to pay for cutting services.

Many of the bands had failed to appreciate that a 7" vinyl record would be played by Disc Jockeys much more often than a demo tape. Hot Knife point out, however, that pressing companies generally are rationalising, due to a long term decline in vinyl record sales overall. This is so despite a greater turnover in the popular music industry where there is more variety, more bands, though in smaller, specialised fields, with the record buying public moving away to some degree from "super" groups, and specialist charts (dances, indie, hip-hop etc) becoming ever more relevant to consumers. In this worst case scenario, say Hot Knife, it is plants which concentrate on pressing vinyl records which will be hardest hit, rather than those who mainly offer cutting facilities.

It is clear that investment in manufacture of tapes, records and compact discs, along with sleeve, insert and label design, would be a step in the right direction. Good local facilities would obviate the need for the production process to be carried on outside the region, usually in the already booming South East, or in other European countries. However both quality control and competition from other, new producers needs urgently to be introduced.

*Retail*

Retailing in the local popular music industry has not generally exploited the possible new technologies and new environments for popular music consumption. It has generally been divided between the impersonal chain store (HMV/Our Price) format and the "indie" record shop (Eastern Bloc, for example). It is the latter which have provided the dynamism, though not the sales volume, of the local popular music economy. Small independent companies have been linked to the shops, Creed in the case of Eastern Bloc in the city centre, which have attained international publicity for their ventures. Radio exposure, especially on local networks, GMR, Piccadilly, Key 103, Sunset and KFM has been significant, as has coverage on television programmes such as "Snub TV".

The situation of Manchester's best known independent record shop Eastern Bloc in the shopping arcade of Affleck's Palace in Oldham Street is also noteworthy. The retailing of various goods and services (clothing, posters, jewellry etc) in close proximity to record shops and coffee bars is a successful precedent that might be followed if an entertainments quarter was considered viable. An embryonic "quarter" exists at 48, Princess Street, where independent labels, label and record sleeve designers, promoters and others rent offices in the same block at reasonable, affordable rents. The desirability of developing more of such premises, possibly with mixed use managed workspace including rehearsal and design studios, was a priority for respondents. Further, if such co-ordination was given priority, technological developments such as computer links could be exploited fully, to build connections between say music production companies in Europe and distributors and concert promoters in Greater Manchester, and vice versa.

*Rehearsal*

Although the situation regarding rehearsal facilities is much better in the Greater Manchester than it was in Sheffield before the development of their Cultural Industries Quarter, more could be provided. Cheap rehearsal studios were seen as an increasingly important part of maintaining the creativity of popular music in Greater Manchester. These facilities could be extended by; use of more community centres for rehearsal and use of more local authority buildings.

*Recording*

Compared to Sheffield, Greater Manchester could be said to be "groaning under the weight" of recording studios. There are two aspects of recording studio provision, nevertheless. One is the question of access to relatively cheap studios ; the other is the issue of excellence for those with the financial backing to demand top quality facilities. There are wide variations in rates charged for studio time and it is certainly possible that a new city centre recording studio with differential facilities and pricing would be welcomed. The Greater Manchester recording studios have to compete with London where there is evidence of over-capacity and a policy of cutting rates and a willingness to make losses to be recouped at a later stage, which leaves regions like Manchester at a distinct disadvantage. There is, then, a major problem of unfair competition as perceived by recording studios in the Greater Manchester area. Such cut throat competition is threatening the viability of the whole recording sector.

A Centre of Excellence would be one solution to the problem. Top of the range recording studio facilities available at a city centre location, with telecommunications link in conjunction with a new city centre venue, was seen as a potentially productive venture by many respondents. On the other hand, there is the question of accessible, cheap recording studios for bands and singers. Two current proposals should be noted.

First, a community recording studio is shortly to open in the Moss Side district of the city. Named Forward Beat Music Technology, it is funded by

£100,000 from Task Force and £95,000 from the Employment Training Scheme. Its major role, at least in the first year, is to provide training for people to become sound engineers. On the same site in Moss Side a P.A. (Public Address) and equipment hire company will operate (see chapter six).

Second, a proposal from local Manchester independent band, Fallover 24, who used to record for the now defunct Ugly Man record label, has been put to obtain finance for their development, including the suggestion that a Hulme community recording studio be funded as part of the financing of the band. Although one source of finance approached, Agency For Economic Development (AED), turned down the proposal on the grounds that "there was too much existing competition in the area", and that they had "subsequently been advised that Task Force are funding a £100,000 16 track recording studio in close proximity", we feel that this may be a proposal worth taking seriously. The Forward Beat Music Technology studio is primarily aimed at training. This would not necessarily rule out the creation of a new open access community recording studio for the Hulme and Moss Side area.

## Conclusion

In conclusion, it is evident that whatever investment is brought to the regions popular music industry, there has to be more co-ordination between private and public sector. Funding from a variety of sources might be obtained to put the recommendations in this report into practice e.g. Enterprise allowance, North West Arts grants, industrial development loans, local authorities, public/private partnership.

Nevertheless, the failure to conceive of the local popular music economy as a viable cultural industry in its own right, with international potential as other media industries reorganise in the 1990s, is common to both public and private sectors. Our recommendations and summary of responses in this report will hopefully have the effect of altering this constraint on development of the sector in the future.

# 5 Local government and cultural policy

*Justin O'Connor*

## Introduction

In this chapter we suggest ways in which local authorities can develop a strategy to deal with the promotion and development of the arts and cultural industries. We examine existing developments in this area and highlight those problems that need to be overcome if an arts and cultural industries strategy is to be fully effective.

Our researchers interviewed Arts Officers; Economic Developments Officers; personnel within Cultural Services, Museums, Galleries and Libraries; Officers in North West Arts; and a wide range of members of the arts and cultural industries community of Greater Manchester.

We stress the economic argument for an arts and cultural industries strategy, both in terms of employment and urban renewal and emphasise that this economic argument can form an essential part of a strategy designed to enhance the quality of life for all in the local area.

Our investigations found that the current level of awareness of the potential of the arts and cultural industries was generally low, and that some local authorities were organisationally ill-equipped to develop and implement an arts and cultural industries strategy. This points to the need for a corporate strategy involving a wide range of local authority departments. We also stress the need for local authorities to involve the private sector and the wider business community in the implementation of some of the recommendations that we make.

The report commences with a series of short, medium and long-term recommendations which must form the central core of any strategy for the arts and cultural industries in the local area and within the region as a whole. Clearly much of the argument relating to the benefits of an arts and cultural industries policy for the local authorities has been made elsewhere in our report and references to these are made in the text.

**Recommendations**

Each local authority (LA) should draw up a strategy for the development of the arts and cultural industries based around a key objective: to maximise the contribution which the arts and cultural industries can make to the economic and social well-being of the locality and wider region.

Such a strategy can only be effectively implemented in terms of corporate provision. Local authorities must develop a corporate network which will effectively co-ordinate the pursuit of a strategy across a range of departments: Arts, Museums and Libraries, Planning, Economic Development, Education, Tourism, Leisure, Training, Finance. Each local authority should set up a working group involving both officers and councillors with specific responsibility for the development and implementation of this corporate strategy for the arts and cultural industries. This group should have sufficient access across a range of departments to allow it to network both within the local authority and with other local authorities. The LA should look to the co-ordination of its strategy with that of developments and initiatives in the region as a whole. It should look to extending and rationalising its links with existing regional bodies dealing with the arts, tourism and economic development.

*Assessing Current Levels of Provision*

The local authorities should conduct a survey of existing local arts and cultural industries activity and provision. This will provide information on four prerequisites, necessary for the further development of cultural policy. First, the needs of local cultural industries and their potential for growth. Second, the extent and adequacy, including gaps in provision, of local facilities/businesses important for the wider development of arts and cultural industries in the area. Third, an inventory to discover the gaps in existing arts and tourist provision in the area and how these can be developed and expanded as part of an integrated arts and cultural industries strategy. Fourth, the scope and success of existing community arts provision and how these can play a part in a strategy for the arts and cultural industries; that is, as important for the physical improvement of the local environment and as central to the identification and participation of the local community in any strategy for the enhancement of the quality of civic life. The above should be accompanied by an audit of existing local authority resources in the light of the above. This would include funding, equipment, property, expertise and training.

*Medium Term Initiatives*

The local authority should develop a locally based "What's on" publication which should include - beyond Arts and Tourist events and venues - live music in pubs and clubs, restaurants/wine bars and any special shopping attractions. The local authority should begin to create a directory of local Cultural Industries and related services, or it should co-operate in creating one jointly with other authorities or a regional body. They should explore the possibilities of such directories being available in electronic form. Such a directory would prove useful in the promotion of cultural industries and would provide companies and other organisations with the facility to network with each other (see chapter one). The local authority should look towards the establishment of a specific brief for the encouragement of local cultural industries.

Business advisers/enterprise counsellors should be made more aware of the potentials and problems of the local cultural industries, and should be used alongside greater provision of locally-based marketing and business information, training schemes, and advise on access to existing or potential grant schemes/development loans.

The local authority should look at how both public and private sectors could cooperate in the enhancement of the local urban environment through the arts. Such an advocacy role must stress the impact of such physical improvements on the growth of civic pride and identification, and how the quality of local life can be important to the success of both local businesses and inward investment. Thus the local authorities should consider two particular initiatives. One, an examination of the feasibility of Percent for Art schemes, whether formal or informal, applicable to public and/or private development. Any such scheme should not detract from the existing arts budget and should be used for the enhancement of the building/development in question. Note should be taken of the recent Arts Council leaflet on Percent for Art. North West Arts are in the process of publishing a Strategy Document on Public Art which should be examined in detail. Two, take a pro-active role in the development of such groups as Partnership Art who aim, through public art sponsorship initiatives, to get local industries involved in the improvement of the local environment, and thus further stimulating local arts and cultural industries. Local authorities can play an important role in advocating such initiatives amongst the local business community.

The advocacy role of the local authority within the local business sector is crucial to any strategy for the arts and cultural industries. This must stress the economic potential of the arts as a cultural industry and clearly argue for private finance in this sector to be seen as investment rather than as charity or sponsorship. Local authorities should thus look at ways of involving the business community in the development of the arts and cultural industries.

*Property-led Initiatives*

Local authorities should look at the implications of Cultural Quarters (see chapter two), Managed Workspace (chapter one) and Mixed-Use Developments (chapters one and two) for local urban centres. Whilst it is acknowledged that each AGMA authority has different needs, problems and potentialities, these building led initiatives can play a central role in the development of a local arts and cultural industries strategy. These initiatives will involve provision by and for a complex network of public, private and voluntary agencies and needs. This demands the maximum possible co-operation and consultation between these agencies within an overall strategic plan. Local authorities should thus examine the possibility of:

- developing city and town centre mixed-use areas, to include exhibition and performance space, arts/resource centres, restaurant/cafe facilities, and retail outlets;
- developing mixed use office/workspace, with a degree of managed facilities and aimed at emergent local cultural industries;
- discovering ways in which community centres can develop their potential role as centres of local activity, by making them genuinely accessible to all sections of the community and by integrating them with other public and private facilities in the area such as libraries, shops, cafes, restaurants, and leisure centres.

*Training*

Arts Officers should be given the training and back-up facilities to respond to an expanded cultural industries brief. Alternatively, a cultural industries officer could be appointed to deal with this aspect of arts development with a brief which would encompass both Leisure and Cultural Services and Economic Development Departments. Short intensive courses in the implications of the arts and cultural industries should be extended to other officers who may potentially be involved in this sector. Seminars should be provided to help raise awareness of local facilities among those working in key service sectors such as taxi-drivers, hotel porters, and shop-workers who together make up an important unofficial local information network.

Local authorities should survey the level and quality of local courses and training programmes related to the arts and cultural industries, courses central to the local arts and cultural industries such as fine arts, design, recording, audio-visual, media communications should be given a much higher level of business advice and enterprise training than currently offered. This increased provision should look towards closer communication between these courses and the relevant local industries (see chapter six).

Local and national training programmes within the arts and cultural industries should be assessed as to their suitability/success in developing the local arts and cultural industries. Any changes or modifications should be integrated within the overall arts and cultural industries strategy (see chapter six). Training programmes within the arts and cultural industries need not be restricted to specific technical qualifications. Attention must be given to the ways in which fine arts, music, drama and dance workshops, basic recording skills etc. can be used to develop confidence, communication skills, initiative and knowledge amongst local people (see chapter six). The local authority should thus assess the role of community centres and community arts projects within an arts and cultural industries strategy. The emphasis on access and participation that should this role could become an important first step in bringing people into contact with wider training and educational possibilities (see chapter six).

*Community Arts and the Cultural Industries*

The local authority should explore the potential contribution of Community Arts projects to an arts and cultural industries strategy; as a source of talent and creativity, a basis for training, and as a crucial channel for participation and access within the arts and cultural industries. The local authority should look into the potential input of Community Arts projects and community centres in public art schemes, street furniture projects and local street performances/carnivals, and to integrate these with any wider strategy for an arts and cultural industries led urban development scheme. Similarly, they should explore the extent to which organisations and groups within these community centred activities can contribute to a democratic planning process for an arts and cultural industries strategy.

## Cultural Policy: Background

*The Arts*

Over the last fifteen years the definition of the arts and arts policies has begun to change radically. There has been a growing awareness that arts activities extend beyond that sphere traditionally marked out for "High Art" and that the arts can touch people's lives in a much more regular and "everyday" manner than the occasional exposure to the sublime heights of European art works. The potential opposition between the great municipal buildings dedicated to Culture and the everyday environment of the majority of the population was increasingly recognised by the Local Authorities, as central government grants were being drastically cut whilst they were being asked to cope with the social and economic effects of recession. It is within this framework that much of the reassessment of the arts took place.

Two developments ensued. First, arts activities increasingly came to be seen as part of local service provision. This service was much wider than the restricted (albeit important) notion of the presentation of "High Culture". The arts could now be seen as providing a focus for participation and developing communication skills; they could stimulate initiative and creativity in everyday life; they could act as aids to education and therapy; and they could provide a focus for community involvement and identification. All this was often set against the background of unemployment, de-skilling, the deterioration of the local environment and the social dislocations consequent upon recession. Second, this extension of the scope of the arts meant that arts activities now draw in a wide variety of agencies beyond the traditional purveyors of "culture". The arts now involve a complex network of public, private and voluntary bodies all competing for some degree of public funding, private sponsorship and private donations.

Under this double impact of the increased scope and complexity of arts provision, the local authorities have begun over the past few years to develop a more systematic approach to the arts.

*The Cultural Industries*

The Local Authorities have however been generally slow to recognise other aspects of this changing conception of the arts. If "High Art" often seemed remote from people's everyday lives it also excluded from its world that multitude of activities known as "popular culture". This was not just because of the fact that it was "popular" but also because the bulk of its activities occurred in the market place, as a commercial activity. The term Cultural Industries is an attempt to articulate the idea that popular cultural activity is also an economic activity (see chapter one).

Whilst recognising the role of a broadened definition of the arts in the provision of local services they have often ignored or failed to act upon the accumulating evidence that, apart from significantly enhancing the quality of life in the locality, this complex cultural industries sector can have significant economic effects (see chapter eight).

The term "cultural industries" is not an attempt to supplant that of "Art" rather to stress that these activities are not simply charities or services requiring public assistance but are a productive sector in their own right, feeding in a number of different ways into the wider local and regional economy. Whilst local authorities have attempted to channel and influence local arts provision in a number of ways, most significantly through the Community Arts movement, they have consistently failed to recognise the economic potential of the cultural industries and the ways in which they can benefit from local policies directed towards their development.

Moreover, local authorities have been generally slow to recognise how these cultural industries can enhance the quality of local life in a wide range of areas, beyond their possibilities for providing employment and generating local economic growth. The Greater London Council was undoubtedly a pioneer in this respect. Although acknowledging a great number of mistakes they embarked upon a strategy designed to develop the cultural industries in the Greater London region as a distinct sector with great economic potential, but which had previously been excluded from local industrial planning.

What is crucial here is that this attempt to stimulate the cultural industries as an economic sector was also part of an overall strategy for arts and culture. That is, any local authority aiming at the enhancement of the quality of life through an arts and cultural policy must acknowledge the role of the commercial market for the cultural industries in such a strategy. As argued in the GLC's Cultural Industries Strategy;

> public cultural policies tended to have "a relatively marginal impact" on consumption of cultural commodities and services, since they has traditionally been directed at activities which could rarely be commercially viable. The report concluded that the only way for the public sector to have an impact "both on economic and employment patterns and on "culture" in its broadest sense" would be to intervene "through and not against the market".

(Franco Bianchini: The Arts and the Urban Regeneration Process in 1980's Britain. Working Paper 7 April 1989. Centre for Urban Studies. Liverpool University).

*Economic Implications of the Cultural Industries*

The economic argument for a cultural industries strategy operates at a number of different levels (see chapters one and eight). This report has underlined for the Greater Manchester region what was already becoming clear in a growing number of studies since the early 1980's; that the arts and cultural industries have a significant role in terms of employment in the local economy. In Greater Manchester this sector has an estimated turnover of £343m per year and provides over 10,000 jobs (See chapter eight).

However, this sector has wider implications than that of the provision of employment. It links in with the question of urban regeneration that has emerged as one of the crucial problems of the 1980s. The 1970s saw growing concern over the effects of the slow decline of the inner city many industrialised nations. The migration of industry, the growth of the suburbs and the development of out of town retail all combined to present a picture of urban decay and social deprivation, where vibrant city and town centres became deserted at night and at the weekend, with the consequent increase of crime and vandalism. Similarly, a certain view of town planning coupled with unrestricted retail development were to create an impoverished urban centre lacking any civic or community focus other then that provided by shopping (see section two). In the context of the decline of the manufacturing base, especially since 1979 and especially in the North West, the employment potentials of the arts and cultural industries are of course welcome. Local authorities can pursue a number of strategies designed to enhance this sector and its employment prospects.

The economic importance of tourism in Britain has been acknowledged for some time now. Tourism is Britain's fastest growing industry. In 1986 its total turnover was £14 billion with almost one million people directly employed. In broad terms every job in the tourist industry gives rise to a further half-a-job elsewhere. The role of the larger towns and cities in this industry has also been recognised. The rise of short-break holidays, the growth of business visiting and the idea of "cultural tourism" has had a great impact on urban tourism. This is reflected in major tourism strategies being developed by cities such as Glasgow (see section seven) and the general rise of the "Heritage Industry".

Each year over 10 million overnight stays are made in Greater Manchester by tourists. By 1988 tourism was worth £218 millions to Greater Manchester, as compared to £100 millions to Merseyside and £250 millions to the West Midlands. (Figures from Getting Ahead in the Tourism Business. A report to GMTLA by L&R Leisure Consultants, 1988). The economic arguments for the importance of the arts and cultural industries in attracting tourists and visitors from within and outside the region are made in section seven of this report. We would emphasise here not just the importance of arts and cultural events in attracting tourism and city centre spending but how the image and feel of a place, crucial to any serious tourism strategy, can be improved by the general profile and "buzz" of a thriving arts and cultural industries sector. The success of Glasgow in turning its image around is based on its promotion of itself as a centre of artistic excellence. The growth of tourism may have certain drawbacks. Some jobs in this sector are low-skilled and low-paid, often short-term and non-unionised. There is also the potential problem of the split between local needs and tourist needs and the political situation this may create. Indeed there could be a degree of local resentment at the town or city offered up as a heritage park (see sections two and seven).

A strategy for the arts and cultural industries provides an integrated plan through which tourism can be developed as part of a wider and longer-term economic development, one that is responsive to the particular skills and creative abilities of the locality. A developed arts and cultural industries sector thus both extends the scope of potential tourism and places tourism development within a more broadly balanced industrial regeneration strategy.

Developments within communication technology have serious implications for the wider competitiveness of Greater Manchester in an international market demanding increasingly sophisticated data exchange systems. (See section three). Local authorities must act to co-operate on a strategy for developing those local industries involved in this sector. A cultural industries strategy could help to ensure that such infrastructural renewal includes social and cultural goals and enhances local media industries.

Evidence from the USA, Europe and other cities in Britain has shown the extent to which the renewal of urban centres can be successfully linked to a strategy for the arts and cultural industries. (see section seven). This strategy would include: the creation of cultural quarters in production and consumption (see chapter two); mixed use developments and space for artists and other cultural producers (see chapters one and two); the development of public art schemes; the promotion of public performances and street entertainments.

All of these help enhance the urban environment, encourage the use of the town/city centres after work hours and create a critical mass of arts and cultural activity that attracts further producers and consumers to the area. The enhancement of the urban environment and the quality of local life through an arts and cultural industries strategy help foster a sense of civic pride and identification. As Myerscough repeatedly found, even those who did not use arts and cultural facilities, such as the Tate, the Liverpool Philharmonic, the Burrel Collection etc., wanted them to be available and the majority of these were willing to see them paid for out of public money (see J. Myerscough Economic Importance of the Arts in Glasgow. Page 154. Policy Studies Institute. 1988).

Those municipal buildings and institutions crucial to the creation of a civic identity in the 19th and early 20th century - the museum, the Gallery, the Library, the Orchestra, the imposing town hall - all these established a focal point for a sense of citizenship, a participatory public ownership. There is no doubt that social, economic, political and cultural changes have meant that this sense of citizenship needs new forms to express itself and participate within, new foci are necessary.

Many US and European cities have arts and cultural industries strategies (see section seven). Many cities in the UK are moving towards such an integrated strategy for the arts, tourism, urban renewal, training and re-skilling and the regeneration of the economic base. A number of these authorities have begun to actively stimulate the arts and cultural industries by taking a lead in the creation of the necessary economic, communication and organisational infrastructures necessary to compete with London and other European cities.

Some cities are attempting to define themselves as national centres for various kinds of cultural industry, entering into direct competition with other regional centres in the UK. Developments in Glasgow, Birmingham, Sheffield, Liverpool, Newcastle and Cardiff indicate the degree of seriousness with which these strategies are being pursued.

Greater Manchester has a number of advantages over these other regions and cities. It is clear that Greater Manchester has the biggest arts and cultural industries sector in the UK outside London. It has a transport infrastructure unrivalled in the UK outside London, allowing greater scope for the expansion of this sector than that possessed by any other UK urban centre. In some respects Manchester has the profile of England's "second city". However the competition is growing and Greater Manchester well behind many other cities in the elaboration of an arts and cultural industries strategy and indeed in the initial process of acknowledging their growth potential. This is beginning to change, but a concerted effort is needed if Greater Manchester is to seize the opportunities offered by its already existing strengths.

The move towards the single European market will be accompanied by a movement towards the regionalisation of Europe. Already European cities are entering into contact, not only with other national governments but also with other City-regions. Barcelona, Lyon, Grenoble, Bologna, Milan, Cologne, Frankfurt, Luxembourg are among the many examples here. This has two implications for Greater Manchester. First, competition for new cultural industries will be increasingly on an international scale and Greater Manchester will have to compete directly against these other cities. Market forces will not decide this alone, a cooperative and coherent strategy involving public and private agencies in a regional context will be an important factor. Second, although the value of a European profile in this process is difficult to quantify it is clearly a major factor. As we have noted already, this civic image is in large measure derived from the vitality and reputation of the local arts and cultural industries. In many of the major European cities arts and cultural industries strategy have gone hand in hand with an arts led regeneration and enhancement of the urban centres. There is an increasing complementarity between this enhancement of the urban environment, the stimulation of local creativity, the cementing of civic pride and the economic and commercial success of the city within the European arena.

## Existing Levels of Structure and Provision in the Region

This section sketches the current structure of provision with a view to identifying problematic areas. Local authority arts provision has traditionally been centred around those civic buildings with a clear public function; libraries, galleries, museums and performing arts venues. However, over the last fifteen years Arts provision has expanded beyond these traditional confines into a wide range of activities and a complex interaction between public, private and voluntary groups. Responsibility for co-ordination, organisation, development and funding these arts activities has been spread across a number of departments and offices. The major departments here have tended to be Education and Leisure and Cultural Services. This has created a number of problems not least of which has been the lack of an overall strategic body for the utilisation of resources and the development of arts provision. Thus, for example, many outreach and community arts programmes are based in education, while the ostensible responsibility for the arts lies with Leisure service. This dispersal makes an audit of resources and provision very difficult. The attempt has barely begun in the Association of Greater Manchester Authorities (AGMA), and there is no doubt that the financing of arts activities across the various departments is hazy to say the least. With responsibility for the Arts located in Leisure Services, arts administration can often fall to officers with experience in sport and recreational activities and often with little or no arts administration experience.

*Recent Developments*

Over the last ten years there has been a growing awareness of the need for an arts policy. This was a complex process, but we can isolate three related developments. First, the growth of the community arts movement and its relationship to new community politics, especially amongst marginalised or discriminated groups. Second, the rapid growth of unemployment meant that "leisure" became an important and pressing matter for the local authorities to address. Third, the abolition of the Greater Metropolitan Authorities saw the local authorities take an increasingly important role at the local level. It became clear that this funding demanded a coherent strategy.

Most Local Authorities have Arts budgets, although in many cases this is a development of the last three years. Their size varies enormously, from relatively large in Manchester and Salford, to very little in some of the regions smaller authorities. These budgets however do not account by any means for the total overall arts spending in the authorities because arts provision is seen as the responsibility of a number of Departments such as Education and Social Services as well as Departments of Leisure and Cultural Services.

*The Role of the Arts Officer*

The creation of an Arts budget and the move towards an arts plan are undoubtedly the partial result of the creation of the post of arts officer in nine of the AGMA authorities. With the exception of Tameside the Arts Officer (AO) is a creation of the last five years. AO posts were advocated by North West Arts, who also gave financial incentives. In a series of interviews with each of the AOs, they expressed a belief that their were several reasons for the response of the local authorities, namely:

- the search for new roles in the face of enforced contracting out of services and the cuts in central government financing;
- the need to co-ordinate existing arts activities in the LA area;
- to encourage the development of a corporate strategy for arts provision;
- to respond to locally defined and expressed need by stressing access along with the promotion of activities not otherwise available;
- responding to precedent - "everybody else was getting one".

Their brief is often felt to be vague, wide-ranging and confused. AOs were appointed to perform a wide variety of tasks within a local government structure that lacked any overall arts strategy. Clearly the status and location of the AO is a key factor in understanding the role of the arts in local authority structures. The AO is charged with the task of developing such a plan, but this is made difficult by the serious lack of financial and political resources. With the exception of Bolton, where there are two AOs and a clerical assistant, seven other LAs have no administrative support for their AOs. Salford is the exception, being well served by six staff.

AOs were appointed at a relatively low grade. They are excluded from key policy committees and their lines of communication with other departments tends to be horizontal, thus failing to network with those higher grade officers in other departments necessary to any corporate strategy. The AO suffers from the low priority attached to the arts which are often seen as peripheral and therefore soft targets for expenditure cuts and thus often subject to revised budgets despite formal commitments to development plans. The result is that in most cases AOs are faced with an increasing diversification of arts provision without the status, the administrative resources or the time to co-ordinate these developments, let alone relate it to an overall corporate plan.

*Arts and the Cultural Industries*

No local authority in Greater Manchester has yet developed a strategy for the arts and cultural industries. Awareness of the potential of the arts and cultural industries is extremely patchy. Often the term Cultural Industry is poorly understood, and the contribution of the Arts to any economic regeneration strategy is seen as entirely marginal. This is often the case with respect to both Arts and Economic Development officers (EDOs), where both tend to feel that neither is in any way central to the concerns of the other. Links between the AO and EDO are unsatisfactory in most of the local authorities. Some authorities have Arts Forums to which Economic or Industrial Development officers may be asked to attend. Usually any such links are accidental, ad hoc or depend on personal initiative and contacts. Ultimately, in most local authorities links between the AO, the EDO and others relevant officers tend to be infrequent, informal and tied to specific project developments.

Again, except for Salford and Manchester, when interviewed the EDOs did not feel that their briefs took in the arts and cultural industries except in the most marginal way, usually in the form of financial contribution rather than any coordinated planning. Even in those local authorities where the arts and cultural industries potential is acknowledged, corporate links tend to be informal or located around specific developments. Salford's better equipped and higher-graded AO, located in Cultural Services, is much further advanced in the process of working towards an integrated arts and cultural industries strategy than any other local authority, with the possible exception of Manchester. Manchester has begun to move in the direction of a cultural industries policy, but at the moment it is still very ad hoc and spread between various departments. The city is in the process of elaborating a plan, but without the fullest possible consultation this cannot succeed. Recently such a planning forum has begun to move the process forward at chief officer level and to bring in a wide range of departments. Some departments still need convincing that these matters have anything more than peripheral interest to their activities. It is clear that a primary task of any arts and cultural industries strategy is vigorous advocacy.

However, it is equally important to stress that many of the AGMA authorities are engaged in some sort of arts and cultural industries project which is beginning to bring a number of different departments together, and that any such advocacy should try to work outwards from such existing networks and initiatives. These networks can emerge from attempts to develop tourism and leisure, from heritage projects, from traditional prestige visual and performing arts, from arts and resources centres, from large urban replanning schemes, from community arts and urban festivals.

A major initiative, developed by Bury Metro Arts through the Policy and Resources Committee is the Metro Arts Centre at Derby Hall. In three phases it will become, beyond the small receiving venue at present, a tourist information/box office; a cafe-bar with a small performance space; a studio-space both for hire and as use as a resource centre for outreach work. This development will involve the private sector along with the public and voluntary sectors.

Stockport is looking towards the creation of an arts centre, possibly in conjunction with a new leisure complex development. They are also looking for areas in which to build offices for arts based industries. They already have Stockport Village as a small scale craft development.

Rochdale has a well developed community arts programme which was successful in promoting the Rochdale festival. There are also plans to create an arts centre and to create a People's History Centre, with a performing arts venue. Rochdale have decided to close down the central museum and art gallery in order to provide space for this, leaving the collection to go on tour. Remaining will be "front-on/shop-front" library provision and an exhibition space which will act as a base for community outreach programmes.

The Wigan Pier development has become the locus for a very informal, but often quite close networking of officers. Policy is concentrated on mainstream arts, especially the Orchestra-at-the-Mill as Wigan's flagship.

Manchester is witnessing a property-driven initiative associated in part with the creation of the Central Manchester Development Corporation. Along with Salford it is facing the problem of developing a strategy to deal with an already well-advanced cultural industries sector.

Salford has developed the Quays project and an ambitious programme of urban redevelopment involving the cultural industries. It is proposed to complete the Quays project with the creation of a performance arts centre, possibly coupled with the relocation of the present Salford College of Technology's Performing Arts Department. It is also considering the development of both an oral history heritage centre and a managed cultural industries workspace. Salford already has a cultural quarter, although this is as yet underdeveloped.

*Cultural Industries and Community Arts*

There is some degree of mistrust on the part of those involved in local arts administration to the idea of an arts and cultural industries strategy. This is understandable given the long struggle to get Community Arts recognised; there is a fear that any policy shift will undermine their successes. Any arts and cultural industries policy must therefore reassure those involved that this is not the case. Advocacy work must stress that arguments for a cultural industries policy is not a disguise for simplistic and politically weighted notions of "efficiency" or "value for money". Emphasis on the economic benefits of the cultural industries should not mean the displacement of social and educational criteria by the economic. It must be stressed that the development of the cultural industries can - and to be successful, must - be complementary to the sense of access and participation attempted by the Community Arts Movement.

The success of any developmental strategy depends on a high level of consultation with those sectors such a strategy is designed to serve. An arts and cultural industries strategy cannot be mechanically applied. It demands consultation with all sections of those involved in the arts and cultural industries. Community consultation is essential, local needs and wants being taken into account. Part of the success of any such strategy is the sense of local identification it produces. This should be begun at the earliest feasible stage of planning.

However, it is important to recognise that communities are not bound strictly to fixed geographical boundaries. Disabled people, for example, would claim to belong to a community geographically dispersed throughout Greater Manchester. The concept of community must not be used therefore to uncritically oppose localised and centralised provision, as if the former would of necessity reach a community more than the latter. Centralised and localised provisions should not be seen as competing for resources, a struggle between "prestige" arts and community arts. Centralised provision can open up the city and town centres to all social groups, enhancing the quality of life for all members of the civic community. Centralised provision may be easily linked to smaller local centres. Resource centres, providing more sophisticated or expensive services/facilities have often be an essential part of an integrated outreach programme. The Bury Metro Arts centre and the old Rochdale Museum and Art Gallery provided good examples of this. The concept of community in an arts and cultural industries policy should then take note of changed patterns of leisure and recreation in the 1980's which have expanded and made more complex our understanding of the civic community.

There is no reason why existing community centres could not be integrated into a local arts and cultural industries strategy. Training, local arts projects, urban improvement and the development of cultural quarters and an extended evening or night-time economy could all become important aspects of the local community centres. They could become genuine centres of day and night-time urban activity, creating a sense of local identification and significantly improving the quality of life.

**Conclusion**

Although we indicate certain developments above which are to be welcomed, nevertheless further development of the economic potential of the arts and cultural industries is hampered by:
- a lack of coherent, corporate strategy;
- a fragmented administrative and financial structure;
- a lack of administrative and political resources among AOs;
- the placing of responsibility for arts development within departments lacking the specific experience and expertise required for arts administration;
- the marginalisation consequent upon the traditional low-grading and lack of understanding of the arts by other departments, often considered a "soft option" for budget cuts;
- the lack of awareness of the significant role that the arts can play in the revitalisation of the local economy and the enhancement of the quality of life in the region.

The main purpose of this chapter has been to suggest ways in which local authority cultural policy can assist in the development of the arts and cultural industries. It stresses the need to develop a corporate strategy to involve the wide range of departments whose areas will overlap an arts and cultural industries policy. This cross departmental networking is crucial, and is especially so between Arts Officers, Economic Development, Leisure and Cultural Services, Education, and Social Services.

Our report points to the many ways in which local authorities can begin to develop the arts and cultural industries. While the local authorities can begin to take some of these initiatives alone, to be fully successful partnership with the private and voluntary sectors is essential.

In tourism, cultural production and consumption, partnership with the local business community can enable projects to come to fruition which otherwise may have foundered due to lack of local authority capital. These joint ventures can be made economically viable and can pass on their economic and cultural benefits to the wider community. This argument must be central to the advocacy role of the local authority, private sector funding should be understood as investment rather than sponsorship.

An arts and cultural industries strategy not only has significant economic benefits for the local community but can also enhance the quality of life. It can help establish and focus a new civic pride and sense of citizenship in a changing economic, social, political and technological environment.

# 6 Issues in education and training

*Linda Dockery*

**Introduction**

This chapter is concerned with providing an indication of the range and variety of courses within the arts and cultural industries in the Greater Manchester region, and to recommend new initiatives in training and education which would complement and underpin the economic growth and expansion of this sector. It is not intended to provide a comprehensive compendium of the major courses available within the Greater Manchester area. It was evident throughout our investigation that the students who are attracted to this field of study do so without any guarantee of future job security and with the realisation that they are entering a highly competitive world. However, applications for such courses are buoyant and the quality of students attracted are of a high calibre. However there appeared to be little strategic planning for the development of training requirements for the industry in the region yet there was a common perception within educational establishments that more resources and finance should be allocated in order to make this possible. Interviews with those within the industry suggested a degree of skepticism about the ability of those concerned with training and education to respond in a positive and prompt way to their needs.

The BBC has a well established corporate in-house training programme which may not be sustainable in the future as its preeminence in the broadcasting field is eroded and there is a considerable reduction in staff. ITV training tends to utilise external sources of training for specific areas of expertise, in addition to any in-house training. Funding for training tends to focus on national training needs although both organisations realise that moves into a more open broadcasting market will necessitate strengthening regional training. A spokesman from Granada stated that it was their policy to positively discriminate in favour of independent broadcasting companies which are based in the North West. The BBC and ITV would be interested in assisting in any independent training production centre in order to have an interest and influence on future direct training skills. They have recognised that one of the benefits of establishing Channel 5 in the region would be to build up the stock of broadcasting skills locally. However, how committed these organisations are to the financing of training has yet to be ascertained. Initially their representation on boards of educational or training organisations , which already exist, or are proposed, should be actively encouraged.

We cite certain Colleges and Departments to illustrate how educational developments may contribute to this industry and assist in its development and economic growth. Whilst our primary task is to illustrate the ways in which education and training can assist the economic potential of the arts and cultural industries we also note the danger of subordinating general educational standards to narrowly defined vocational training. If the culture industry is to engage in debate regarding the nature of future course provision it will have to be aware of the concerns of the validating bodies such as the Council for National Academic Awards and the Business and Technical Education Council. Similarly, validating bodies have recognised that:

> Feedback from graduates, the observations of other institutions and comments of the industry itself would be valuable in helping staff reassess the balance and structure of courses in relation to their aims and objectives. (statement from CNAA Briefing paper to conference on media education and changing needs of the broadcasting industry).

Many of the courses on offer within Greater Manchester in Art/Design/Communications have a primary concern with the advancement of their attendant skills as a socially desirable pursuit, irrespective of their economic potential. It is not the intention of this section to dwell on the intrinsic value of a cultural, artistic, and literate community, although it will be evident that the impact of a heightened awareness of the "arts" manifests itself in future demand, and this itself leads to increased employment opportunities in all areas of the culture industry.

Arts and Cultural industries also offer an avenue of escape for the long term unemployed where they may pursue particular talents which have never received formal training. This should be recognised and education and training provided which may build upon cultural expression which in turn could be developed into wider work opportunities. Attention must be given to the ways in which fine art, music, drama and dance workshops, basic recording skills etc, can be used to develop confidence, communication skills, initiative and knowledge amongst unemployed people. If access and participation is to be encouraged the means by which courses recruit and operate may have to be reexamined.

**Recommendations**

After extensive interviews with educational institutions in the region and with representatives from the industry, this research recommends that a regional cultural industries training forum should be established in order to bring together representatives of;

Tertiary Educational Institutions
Local Authorities
North West Arts
Greater Manchester Economic Development Ltd
Technical Enterprise Council.

We recommend that the Forum's brief include discussion of:

*The Needs of Industry*

The means and methods of cross co-operation and communication so that educational bodies can be appraised of the needs of the industry. The Cultural Industries are faced with the long term prospect of skill shortages particularly in the area of broadcasting skills as the traditional duopoly of the major broadcasting institutions, the BBC and ITV, is broken up by 1992.

*The Changing Face of Education*

How the industry is made aware of new educational initiatives, such as the credit and transfer scheme at Manchester Polytechnic and how it can take part in the development of courses to meet it's needs.

*The Sharing of Resources and Expertise*

In what ways educational institutions can rationalise their demands for resource intensive courses and consider partnerships and joint bids for external funding or co-operation with the establishment of any proposed North West Media Training Centre.

*The Development of Community Initiatives*

How community initiatives in the field of training such as the Moss Side Forward Beat Music Technology Centre could be further encouraged to provide those in the local community with the opportunity to develop skills and talents relating to the cultural industries.

*The Need for Short Course Provision at a Cost-effective Rate*

The requirement of auditing current course provision, and the means by which practioners and professionals within the industry and Colleges of Further and Higher Education can develop new courses which incorporate the needs of the industry. This short course provision should be extended to include the training for local authority officers who are concerned with their local cultural industries. Local community centres could usefully assist in bringing in those who are involved with the key service sectors in order to increase their awareness of local activities through information seminars.

*Linkages with the new Technical and Enterprise Councils*

The establishment of an essential link with the new Technical and Enterprise Board so that significant representation with regard to education and training in the arts and cultural industries is ensured.

**Training and Education: Background**

The Greater Manchester region is home to the BBC and Granada, large broadcast institutions with in-house production. Therefore any forum for the Greater Manchester region should seek representation from these institutions. In addition, as the result of the traditional 'duopoly' of broadcasting being broken down, other organisations within this sector will need to be consulted. With the likely multiplicity of broadcasting sources in the 1990s, it is expected that there will be consequences on the structure and nature of employment.

In a recent Council for National Academic Awards publication this validating body acknowledged that young people in the future would be less likely than in the past to go into one institutional form of broadcasting as employees for their entire career. They would be more likely to be working on short-term contracts on a freelance basis, as the recruitment and training policies of broadcasting institutions changed. These changes will have implications for media education currently offered in Polytechnics, Colleges and Universities. Representatives from educational establishments need to be invited in order that a genuine dialogue can be encouraged and information obtained on new initiatives within the education field on the development of courses and the availability of resources in terms of staff and equipment. Different colleges should be able to contact this forum to establish whether there were opportunities for sharing equipment or making joint bids for funding. Technical advances, particularly in the field of the audio/visual medium is such that with the present financial position of many educational establishments they would simply not be able to keep abreast of the new developments in equipment. It would therefore be rational to consider a central workshop which could provide items of equipment and technical expertise which could be hired or bought by several institutions.

Industrial representatives on the forum would be informed of new educational undertakings which would enable greater access to short courses and at the very least provide instruction on the mechanics of the validation process for higher level qualifications. Regional training initiatives could be identified within the creative and technical areas of the cultural industries and could be more readily linked to commercial initiatives. In this way the forum could provide a focus for matching short and long term training requirements to policy decisions on regeneration schemes which include the provision of further cultural industries or the expansion of present ones.

Local authority representatives could express their concerns regarding the need to build in training for their officers in order to increase the awareness of the implications of the arts and cultural industries for the local communities. The whole area of increasing short course provision could be examined in order to increase business advice and enterprise training for various groups including arts administrators and 'artists'. The concerns of the unemployed could be represented, particularly with regard to the links such a forum would wish to establish with the new Training and Enterprise Councils. It would provide an effective lobby for representations to the Training and Enterprise Councils and ensure that training in the Arts and Cultural industries were considered for development initiatives.

*Industry's View of Education*

In order to establish new courses or develop new areas within courses, educational establishments need to engage in elaborate processes of monitoring and validation. Those lacking experience in the world of education are often frustrated at the length of time it takes to develop courses. In a recent briefing paper produced by the CNAA for their conference on the pattern of media education and the changing needs of the broadcasting industries it was recognised that it could speed up its response to the changing environment in which students in media and communications were preparing for work.

The needs of organisations such as the BBC and ITV together with independent producers within the broadcasting field are diverse. They cover a spectrum of educational requirements including the acquisition of specific technical training, the general graduate qualities which extol the virtues of educational attainment and general aptitude, to an emphasis on wider access and equal opportunity policies associated with the accreditation process of the ACTT. The emergence of new training centres such as the London School for Performing Arts and the North East Media Training Centre reflect a concern with developing close relationships between training and employment.

*The London School for the Performing Arts and Technology* has been part-funded by the British Phonographic Industry and is part of the Government's City Technology Programme. It's site will be shared with Croydon College, providing possible opportunities for collaboration with the local tertiary education system. Funds are raised by British Phonographic Industry Trust members and sponsorship arrangements for much of the equipment for the school are currently being sought with electronics groups around the world. Kenneth Baker, Secretary of State for Education, commenting on the funding of the school commented,

> I am delighted that we and the music industry are co-operating in this exciting educational initiative, helping to secure a pool of talent for all aspects of the entertainment industry - one of the country's most successful export earners. (British Record Industry Trust Press Release on the proposed opening of the London School for the Performing Arts and Technology).

The possibility of a similar school for the region could be explored by the Forum in consultation with interested parties within industry and education.

*The North East Media Training Centre*

A recent training guide produced by the North East Media Development Council, which was concerned with the prospective trainees of the film, video and television industries, contained an overview of types of courses available nationally. Manchester was notable in its absence - despite the fact that it is a major educational centre..

The North East Media Development Council was established in 1984 to help the region and the economy of North East England obtain the full benefits of the developing telecommunications, video and computing technologies. It acknowledged a growing market for independent programme makers and its attendant growth in the social, cultural and educational role for film and television. This Training Centre is funded by the five local authorities in the region and is a professional film and video training centre with two broadcast standard television studios incorporating advanced audio equipment and staffed by specialist tutors with technical and administrative back-up. The Centre aims to recruit members of groups to whom training is often denied and who are both "under and misrepresented in and by the media industry at present". These include women, ethnic minorities, people with disabilities and people with no formal qualifications.

An important determinant of the link between training courses and the industry is ACTT accreditation. In order to work in most sectors of the film, video and television industry, it is necessary to be a member of the ACTT. Therefore a place on an accredited course is advantageous in terms of it leading to employment, although it is not a guarantee. For a course to be accredited, it has to meet certain standards and guidelines determined by the ACTT. Discussions should take place with the ACTT in any local authority initiative to establish a similar institution in the Greater Manchester area.

Within the Greater Manchester region Salford College of Technology's Department of Performing Arts and Media Studies are in consultation with the local authority regarding the establishment of a Performing Arts Complex at Salford Quays. This complex would offer band musicianship in addition to theatre, dance, media, recording, video and film. This might be combined with tourist attractions such as a National Band Centre and Museum of Sound incorporating research elements involved with electronic music recording, electro-acoustic music, film and radio music archives.

The department, currently situated in the Adelphi Building, is short of accommodation. It maintains a high level of technological based equipment together with recording and electro-acoustic studios. It has recently introduced a new HND BTEC in Media Production as well as its established BTEC National Diploma in Media and Communication Techniques and plans to run a BA Degree in Production/Performance, and a Higher National Diploma in Performance. The Department sees itself as the alternative College for performance and media with its BA in Band Musicianship; a Higher National Diploma in Popular Music; a Graduate Diploma in Band Musicianship; a Diploma in Music; and a College Higher Certificate in Band Musicianship.

In establishing a form of new Performing/Media Art Institution it would be unrealistic for the whole of Salford College of Technology's Department of Performing Arts and Media Studies to be transposed wholly and uncritically into a new Northern Centre for Performing Arts. Nevertheless, the Department could contribute to such an initiative given its experience in the field of Popular Music education.

Currently, there are seven film and video courses in England and Wales which carry ACTT accreditation, the majority are located in the South East of England. The North East Media Development Council has receives support from bodies such as the five local authorities of the region; Northern Arts; the British Film Institute; the European Social Fund; the City Action Team; the Urban programme; the Tudor Trust; the association of Cinematograph, Television and allied Technicians and the Manpower Services Commission. It is not certain how secure these sources of finance are given the resource intensive nature of such courses but if a similar scheme for the North West was considered by the proposed forum, collaborative ventures with Manchester Polytechnic or Salford College of Technology could be investigated. Part of the forum's brief should be to investigate to what extent the film, video and television industry could usefully exploit the facilities such a centre would offer in the way of providing refresher courses for professionals in the industry.

*Industry-led Training*

There is a growing awareness that in order for industry to meet the growing demand for the forecasted shortage of labour skills in the 1990s it will have to make financial contributions for its training. If training and education is promoted as an additional benefit to a company then employers will be more likely to accept that a contribution or "levy" should be made by them. An interesting development in the "levy" system is operated through JOBFIT.

*JOBFIT* (Joint Board for Film Industry Training) is the first systematic industry-wide training scheme for new entrants to ACTT technical grades in the freelance sector. The scheme is sponsored by the ACTT (Association of Cinematograph, Television and Allied Technicians), the AFVPA (Advertising Film and Video Producers' Association), the BFTPA (British Film and Television Producers Association), IPPA (Independent Programme Producers Association) and Channel 4. It is funded by a levy on all film productions made under the agreements between the ACTT and the Employers' Associations. It's "apprentices" gain a thorough grounding in all aspects of film making and receive a training allowance during their two years of training. JOBFIT is committed to an equal opportunities policy and half the intake are women while one-third come from ethnic minority groups. JOBFIT always anticipated developing training outside London but their first priority has been to establish a secure and successful base from which to expand the training provision. The training is specific to technical and production grades of film-making and trainees are attached as supernumeraries to crewing levels on a variety of film productions and departments. Throughout the two years, on-the-job experiences are supplemented by hands-on training in the form of short courses at recognised film and television training centres. A recognised film and television training centre which could be identified within Manchester would have the opportunity to develop the contacts so necessary within this industry. The proposed forum should examine whether JOBFIT could be usefully applied to training needs in the region.

*The Future for Colleges of Further and Higher Education*

The region's Colleges of Further and Higher Education are funded by a new body, the Polytechnics and Colleges Funding Council (PCFC). This allows a greater degree of flexibility in managing financial affairs and encourages an entrepreneurial approach towards independent funding. It is already evident that some are responding to the demands made on them by locally based industry and staff involved in the teaching programmes of the University/Polytechnic and Colleges of the region also work in consultative capacities. Industry should be made more aware of new educational initiatives, such as the credit and transfer scheme at Manchester Polytechnic, and should take part in the development of short courses to meet specific needs. Colleges of Further and Higher Institutions should consider their recruitment policies for the appointment of staff to strategic managerial roles acknowledging the increasing need to compete for external funding.

*Manchester Polytechnic:* Colleges will need to put more energy into the pursuit of industrial clients. At Manchester Polytechnic there is at present an exhibition of the Design Council's work and its implications for the single European Market in 1992. The Design Council approached the Polytechnic and despite the fact that this exercise is promoting London based design companies the Faculty of Art and Design, by exhibiting student projects at the same time, will be exploiting this avenue for promotion. Currently ten student placements within the design industry have been created as a direct result of this event. The Polytechnic has shown itself to be aware of the new demands being made with regard to financial independence and has taken steps to encourage new initiatives in the area of enterprise. It was was one of the first of eleven higher education institutions to receive funding to develop programmes of training students in enterprise. These programmes will run over five years, after which it is hoped that an enterprise component will be introduced into its courses. These enterprise activities will be embedded into courses and will involve an external client who will be consulted on the assessment part of the enterprise training. As part of their enterprise training several students have been placed with a major advertising firm in a work-shadowing capacity. It is hoped that the knowledge and skills developed in this work situation will enable them to convert their knowledge into consultative abilities for the students of the School of Theatre.

A second interesting development is the Credit Accumulation and Transfer scheme (CAT) based on CNAA guidelines which is being developed through the Polytechnic's Academic Board. The operational methods are not yet determined but the indications are that it could prove to be an advantageous method of recruitment to a more flexible mode of access to study, not least in the Art/Design and Performance fields. A CAT scheme has two major aims: to give credit for learning wherever it occurs, provided it can be assessed; to give the opportunity to vary the pace, mode and pattern of study. These aims are achieved through credit accumulation and credit transfer. Initiatives in this field indicate that Colleges of Further and Higher Education are aware that there is a need to develop the acquisition of credit to encourage the updating of skills and knowledge throughout professional life. Interestingly, this scheme attempts to give credit for learning prior to registration; students can join courses with advanced standing, credits being obtained from employment based learning and professional bodies. This will lead to closer co-operation with employers, other institutions, and distance learning centres. It also provides employers with the opportunity to identify pathways to meet specific training needs, and enables the Polytechnic to market accredited units as short courses, continuing education, and professional updating programmes. Students should find that there is increased flexibility and choice, particularly for part-time mature students, and accreditation for prior experiential learning. The credit and transfer system will enable a programme of study to be jointly designed by the Polytechnic and the employer. Students will be able to follow units, whose programme they can determine, and which will be tailored to the needs of their employer. Through other colleges participating in the same programme CAT will enable both an exchange of ideas and resources. The benefits for the Polytechnic include the generation of income from licensing, consultancy and general course management fees; staff development through contact with industry in a secondment capacity and consultancy; and the building of a firm base for future recruitment.

In addition to the educational fields of audio/visual media the Forum would be appraised of the opportunities in the area of fine art and design. For instance the Art and Design Faculty of Manchester Polytechnic is the largest in the country and offers a wide range of courses for 1,500 students on full-time and sandwich courses. The staff have built a good relationship with industry and many "live projects" are set by industry. Many of the staff have had work experience within the industry and the Faculty is an acknowledged Centre of Excellence.

Students can enrol for courses ranging from foundation to post-graduate higher degrees in Fine Art. Opportunities for industrial contact could be strengthened by an introduction to what is available in courses such as the Graphics Technology Courses - B.Sc. and B.Sc.(Hons) combined studies with printing and photographic technology options or the textiles/fashion degree with chief studies in embroidery, fashion or printed and woven textiles. The Department of three dimensional design offers M.A.s in industrial and interior design and its degree includes three areas of chief studies for potential graduates in wood/metal/ceramics; industrial design; and interior design. The Department of Fine Art has excellent facilities for drawing and painting and a large and well equipped studio/workshop for sculpture (providing facilities for wood, metal, plastics, carving, modelling, moulding) a spray shop and a large foundry for bronze casting. The Faculty, whilst encouraging contracts for commissioned work would be anxious to protect its students from exploitation or 'getting something on the cheap' and collaborative projects with industry would have to be seen as part of the educative process.

*Stockport College of Technology - The Department of Design:* This department provides an example of changes made to attract industry into consultative course development. The department runs a number of BTEC National Diplomas as well as a BTEC Higher National Diploma in Design. Their HND course in Design is of a hybrid nature with an emphasis on computer graphics, and applications are buoyant.

An awareness of design has swept through the UK in recent years with revolution in the retail business, the impact of advertising, and the growth of the communications industry. Ninety three per cent of the students from the Design Department of Stockport College were recruited into full-time employment on completion of their courses, and in one of the most prestigious of competitions, the Creative Design Awards, Stockport students enjoyed considerable success. The course leader of the Textile Surface Pattern BTEC National Diploma aims to use the Department of Design at Stockport as an agency working with industry; to design for printed surfaces as well as specialising in design and production of machine knitted garments. It is her intention that the students provide garments for sales promotions, pattern books, exhibitions and publicity literature, together with the staging of fashion shows.

Manchester's potential as a design centre has not been appreciated, and as such it looses many of its most enthusiastic graduates to London, and other centres in Japan and Italy. Glasgow is planning a major Design Centre in the Merchant Quarter of the city, and hopes to become what was described to us as, "a mini Milan". Yet the traditional industries of the textile world are here in the Greater Manchester region.

*Royal Northern College of Music* is acknowledged to be a national centre of excellence in the field of Classical Music education. Its facilities are excellent - the BBC take advantage of their recording equipment. The college also sees itself as an Arts Centre and is open in the evenings and at weekends as a venue for commercial usage. An external marketing agency is employed to promote the college together with a promotions co-ordinator to attract sponsorship. The college mounts public events and concerts throughout the year, such as the BBC Young Musician of the Year, and hires out its facilities to visiting and touring companies. It also offers facilities to community organisations and recently joined with the Green Room to co-promote Ethnic Artists. The demand for use of the facilities is oversubscribed but Arts events in themselves do not provide the income that the College's involvement as a conference provider does.

*The Sharing of Resources and Expertise*

Educational Institutions should rationalise their demands for resource intensive courses and consider partnerships and joint bids for external funding. They might also consider co-operating in the establishment of any proposed North West Media Training Centre. Institutions of further and higher Education should consider sharing the cost of expensive items of equipment which are not in constant use and creating an environment whereby it would be possible to 'share' or 'rent' equipment from each other.

Stockport College of Technology's Department of Design, Blackpool College, and Manchester Polytechnic have combined to purchase a Quantel - a digital paintbox state of the art graphic design tool. The three institutions made a successful application to the Department of Education and Science for funding because of the cost of this equipment. It was a sucessful application and the equipment is being shared and used by the three institutions.

By attracting external funding to separate departmental accounts departments can exercise a degree of control over financing further innovatory ventures. The co-operation necessary to the success of the above application has brought the additional benefit of forging links between ties institutions so that now Stockport students will be directed towards the Polytechnic for higher level studies.

Both Manchester University and the Polytechnic have recognised the need to develop the resource base for courses concerned with media/film/T.V. and video production to ensure that their future students will be literate in those mediums. However, the funding necessary to satisfy those requirements for each educational institution would be enormous. There would be advantages in the creation of a regional centre which could supply the facilities, share the cost of up-dating such equipment, and provide the necessary technical staff to maintain it.

*The Development of Community Initiatives*

Community initiatives in the field of Training such as the Moss Side Recording Studios Project could be further developed and encouraged. The Forward Beat Music Technology Centre, which is being part-funded by the Moss Side/Hulme Task Force will provide training for students in studio engineering. Their training program provides a widely recognised qualification for studio engineers and trains those who are interested or involved in other musical fields such as producers, writers, and musicians.

To set up the project, Employment Training contributed £95,000 and Moss Side-Hulme Task Force contributed £100,000 for capital expenditure. Some private sector input such as reductions on the cost of recording equipment is also expected. Upon completion of the studio engineering course a student will have a B-Tec 1st Diploma after one year with an option to complete another year for a B-Tec 2nd Diploma. The organisers of this course feel there is a growing demand for this type of training. Popular music itself is becoming increasingly more technical, and they know of no other studio that fills the needs of the public in the same way. The centre will have an Employment Training Manager acting as an administrative body to oversee activities, 6 members of staff to train and guide students and 30 trainees per year. Some of these trainees are already working musicians and\or writers but need further training and a qualification. The training is a combination of theory based training at Central Manchester College, practical work at the studio, and work placement.

In the same building as Forward Beat but run as a separate business will be a public address company. This public address company will hire equipment along with an engineer for various productions. It will also be able to offer rehearsal rooms for bands to hire. The public address company will be able to take on some students on work placement schemes. Allowing students to help set up P.A. equipment for various venues and events will provide valuable knowledge that can only be taught by "hands on" experience. In choosing trainees they are looking for a mix of people who are currently active in the music business as well as those who have no experience but do have a keen interest in the subject. Hopefully the trainee will already have a channel in which to direct his skills e.g. one prospective trainee is already a sound engineer with a local band but needs further training. Forward Beat is not attempting to specialise in, or direct the students towards any particular type of music. Interest in any kind of music is encouraged including acid house, hip hop, regge, pop, and jazz. The organisers see Forward Beat Music Technology Centre evolving into a base where people can telephone or visit for general advice; workshops can be held; and hopefully that it will operate as a nationally recognised training organisation. They would like the P.A. company to expand and to eventually organise large concerts and could, in the future, expand on pre-production recording by providing writing facilities, demos etc. This would allow musical talent to be expressed that may have previously gone unnoticed due to lack of funds. Future plans also include hiring out both the Public Address system and the studio when not in use for Employment Training. It may also be possible to run short (5 day) courses in sound engineering for interested parties.

North West Arts has been active in several areas of education and training in the Arts. Counter Image, Manchester's film, video and photography workshop, worked on a photography project with primary schools in Greater Manchester. Cornerhouse, the city's film and exhibition centre, runs extensive education programmes in conjunction with their exhibitions. Stockport Art Gallery's photography commission 'Making Tracks' was awarded to Greg Leach, who as well as producing a new collection of photographs is working with Stockport College and local Schools.

At the Abram Moss Centre, part of the North Manchester Community College, a successful community music project has been running for two years and is now recognised as an important community resource. Indeed, Abraham Moss Centre was chosen as the location for the first national community music conference. The conference, funded and organised by North West Arts resolved to form an Association of Community Musicians and to make the conference an annual event.

Community arts projects can serve as a basis for training and as a focus for participation and access to the arts and cultural industries. Local authorities should look into the potential input of Community Arts projects and community centres in public art schemes, street furniture projects and local street performances.

*The Need for Short Course Provision*

Institutions of further and Higher Institutions within the Greater Manchester region should consider providing short courses to help artists with basic business skills. North West Arts' initiatives in this field have centred on the Centre for Arts Management, which is based at Liverpool University. This Centre has been set up jointly by NWA, Merseyside Arts, and the Arts Council. The courses, drawn up after consultation with arts workers in the region, include courses in marketing, planning, business awareness, financial management and information technology, as well as racism awareness and equal opportunities.

In the field of Art and Design there has been a tendency to disparage the world of business. The "Artist's Artist" is often symptomatic of an educational world still embracing the conditions of the Art Colleges of the 50s and 60s - when London Art Galleries were the only outlets for an artist's work. The philosophy of being grant-aided indefinitely in order to remain "pure" is still a common expectation.

*Art Administrators*

There are courses available nationally to train Arts Administrators at Leicester Polytechnic, Liverpool Polytechnic, Newcastle-upon-Tyne Polytechnic and the City University. Courses offered to Administrators already acting in that capacity should be developed after consultation with the proposed client base. Theatre Administrators in the North West are currently applying to the Arts Council for funding to provide short courses in conjunction with the Centre For Arts Management. They are hoping to match this funding to allow for staff development to take place. They believe that courses offered in the past have been pitched at too low a level.

The ten theatres that have come together in making this bid to the Arts Council all found that they had common training needs with regard to every level and expertise of their staff from lighting engineers to stage managers. There was a suggestion from one of the Administrators that Marks and Spencer PLC might be interested in supporting a scheme of mutual co-operation where the theatres could feed into their training schemes. This could be developed further given the present attempts to attract business into sponsoring the Arts. Theatres could approach businesses to see if members of their staff could attend training sessions that companies in other commercial sectors currently undertake.

Recently a four-part business training course, organised by North West Arts and ABC Consultants of Hyde focused on marketing and planning and was well attended by arts organisations in the region, as were three seminars on aspects of marketing organised by NWA's Marketing Department. North West Arts are keen to develop a strategic approach to media training in the region and produce a media resources directory.

Arts officers within the Local Authority network should be given training to respond to any expanded cultural industries brief and short intensive courses in the implications of the arts and cultural industries should be extended to other officers who may potentially be involved in this sector, as argued in section five of this report

*Linkages with the new Technical and Enterprise Councils*

The proposed forum should establish the essential link with the new Technical and Enterprise Boards which are about to be established within the region in order that significant representation with regard to training in the arts and cultural industries is ensured. In a recent report by Comedia Consultants (1989), it was noted that Trades Unions in the industry, particularly the ACTT and

BETA, have been involved in various programmes for skills-based training. They are now attempting to co-ordinate training provision through the Training Federation. These efforts are aimed at influencing the move towards standardised vocational training through the Training Commission sponsored National Council for Vocational Qualifications. Comedia mention the new Training and Enterprise Councils as a possible avenues for influencing the quality, objectives and content of training programmes, with the advent of this employer-led initiative. It has yet to be established how the new TECs for the Manchester region will be influenced with regard to its employer Board members. Now, whilst the Boards are in the development stage, is an ideal opportunity for representations to be made to ensure that the educational and training requirements of the culture industry are not overlooked.

## Conclusion

The aim of this chapter has been to indicate the ways in which education and training provision can become more responsive to the requirements of the culture industry. We have examined a number of initiatives, local and national, in order to establish the issues that should be debated within a regional forum. These issues can be summarised as follows. First, discussion is needed to establish the ways by which educational institutions can help meet the needs of the culture industry. The development of short course provision to meet specific training needs is one way in which this can be accomplished. Second, within the educational sphere, and given the rapid technological change associated particularly with the media and audio-visual industries, we feel that educational institutions should examine ways of sharing such technology. Third, in keeping with our conception of the culture industry and the development of employable skills within local communities, community initiatives in local training should be encouraged. Allied to the above we feel it imperative to establish links with the new TEC's in order to set the agenda for educational and training initiatives required by the culture industry. Finally, given the reassessment taking place in higher education we believe it is an opportune moment to develop links with key figures within the arts and cultural industries sector. It will be crucial that the appropriate interested parties are identified so that meaningful discussion can occur.

# 7 Urban regeneration and the arts

*Derek Wynne*

**Introduction**

Economic importance studies of the arts and cultural industries have or are currently being conducted in many major cities. They are seen as a necessary prerequisite to the development of plans for economic and urban regeneration. The primary concerns of research and consultancy work in this area centre around five interelated issues. First, the use of the arts as a vehicle for urban regeneration. Second, the development of and continued support for the cultural industries in recognition of their increasing economic importance. Third, the protection and fostering of the arts and artists in cities where continued commercial development has forced arts activity and artists out of revitalised 'downtown quarters' which they, in part, have helped to create by their initial presence and, importantly, can continue to sustain. Such 'protection and fostering' recognises the arts as an important and necessary part of the urban infrastructure. Fourth, the development of strategies to encourage 'cultural tourism' which is increasingly being recognised as a major ingredient in local economies. Fifth, an examination of the contribution that the arts make to the personal development and well being of the population.

The results and consequent development from the work described below has seen the creation of a number of projects which fall into four categories. One is the establishment of public and private sector partnerships for arts led urban regeneration projects between local government, arts associations, development agencies, property developers and organisations representing local commercial interests. A second has seen the redevelopment of local government cultural policy. A third project has been the creation of cultural quarters or areas in which a 'critical mass' of arts activities is actively encouraged. Finally, we can observe strategies for encouraging the business expansion and maintenance of cultural industries through affordable residential, studio and workshop provision.

Together these strategies have produced a variety of practical responses such as:

*Mixed use,* managed workshop, property led development.

*The establishment of fashion, design, craft and audio-visual centres* in which cultural producers can show their work to prospective clients, and in some cases retail to consumers.

*The creation of 'arts centres'* which contain not only facilities for service provision and education, traditionally associated with the local authorities and/or voluntary associations, but also facilities for professional and semi-professional cultural production, and associated administrative functions.

*Public and private sector programmes* for public art, environmental art and sculpting, street furniture renewal and landscape beautification.

*The construction of 'cultural tourist' trails* and associated promotional and educational literature taking visitors and residents alike on a tour through both time and space via a conceptual and in some cases physical reconstruction of an areas past or heritage. It should be noted here that Manchester/Salford leads the way via the creation of Europe's first inner-city heritage site ie Castlefield.

*The establishment of distribution networks and marketing services* through which local cultural producers can establish wider markets.

*The establishment of the spectacle* through imaginative architectural production(s).

*The establishment of institutions of national and/or international importance* such as art galleries, museums, and or performing arts facilities locating companies with national/international reputations.

*The co-ordination of arts festivals and theme weeks* throughout the year to provide cultural animation programmes for both the local public and visitors

*obtaining the location of international arts and sporting events,* with the latter producing its own associated cultural programmes.

**Background Information**

Here we examine developments in other towns and cities in other parts of the world, principally North America and Europe, together with reporting on more specific developments elsewhere in the UK. It is felt that it is particularly important to locate such development in the international context given the following factors. First, Manchester's undoubted status as a city of international dimension. Second, the increasingly international nature of cultural tourism, in which the arts play a major part. Third, the importance of developing the regions' profile, and therefore Manchester's central role in that profile, as regional rather than national boundaries come to the fore. This will be especially so in a Europe, which if not federal, will certainly take on an increasingly regional context as the open market approaches, and the European Parliament increases its involvement in regional issues. Fourth, the extent to which the arts and cultural industries can be used to attract inward investment; both in their own development, and in other sectors of the regional economy.

The rest of this chapter begins with an overview of the work undertaken from which this part of the report has been produced, and then examines developments in other towns and cities individually, bringing these together in a concluding summary at the end.

*Developments Elsewhere: What Other Cities Have Done*

Here we provide details of some of the developments that have taken or are taking place in other cities and towns. For purposes of brevity only the most pertinent developments are examined in detail. Where similar developments have taken place elsewhere, these are noted in the text.

*Toronto, Canada:* In many ways the City of Toronto and its surrounding metropolitan area provides an example, of a city similar in scale to the Greater Manchester area itself. In addition, it has gone through, and is currently experiencing some of the problems faced by Manchester. Even more interestingly, although not exactly mirrored, it contains many similar organisations, and a government structure that bears some resemblance to that of the Greater Manchester region. Its Harbourfront Corporation is not dissimilar to the Central Manchester and Trafford Park Development Corporations. It contains a waterside frontage similar in many ways to Salford Quays and the river and canal basins, in which the problems of industrial decline and dereliction are also being tackled in somewhat similar ways. Finally, although again, not exactly mirrored, it has an Arts Council whose functions are very similar to those of North West Arts. Inevitably there are dissimilarities, the chief being, for our purposes, Toronto's position in Canada's arts and cultural productions hierarchy, where it is definitely placed at the top. In contrast, Manchester, competing with other UK regional centres, inevitably comes a very poor second, third or fourth to London, this position being dependent upon what one wishes to emphasise in comparison with the other UK regional centres. However one chooses to measure these factors, all come a very poor second to London, itself one of the major cultural capitals of the world.

The two most pertinent examples of the treatment of Toronto's arts and cultural industries can be seen in the work undertaken by the City Council and Toronto Arts Council to encourage the continued development of the arts and cultural industries, and the activities of the Harbourfront Corporation.

Each of these organisations have a degree of responsibility for the arts and cultural industries and Toronto Arts Council is regarded as the agency possessing the necessary expertise in such matters as provision and development. The Toronto Arts Council, unlike NWA is a City Council initiative which receives funding from the city and provincial and federal government, and the Canadian Arts Council. Its everyday working relationships are much closer to the city council than to the Canadian Arts Council, and it sees itself as acting in the interests of the arts and artists for and of Toronto. As such it is able to mobilise the support of the arts community, councillors and relevant council departments in fulfilling and expanding the role played by the arts in the city and metropolitan area. Its profile concerning professional artistic development is much higher than that of NWA and certainly higher than that of the arts officers in the AGMA Local Authorities, the latter, in particular, seeing their role as one of arts provision in community development and outreach (arts education) projects.

Major studies pertaining to the development of Toronto's arts and cultural industries undertaken by the Toronto Arts Council in conjunction with Toronto City Council include: 'Cultural Capital: an economic importance study of the arts and cultural industries in Toronto' (1985); 'No Vacancy: the care and feeding of Toronto's artists' (1988). This study examines the residential and workspace problems associated with the major commercial and financial centre developments in Toronto over the past ten years and has helped in the formulation of the City's Cultural Policy. Both studies have resulted in vigorous activities on behalf of the artistic community. Developments resulting from these analyses include the following. First, residential/studio-workspace projects, and the creation of Artspace, an organisation to foster development, manage and administer these. Second, the establishment of a TV and Film commission by the City council to encourage the use of Toronto by the TV and Film industry. Third, the incorporation of art and sculpture in building development projects.

*Toronto Harbourfront* is a federal initiative, established in the early seventies, but one which has only begun to take shape in the last ten years. Although not directly equivalent to the UDC's its activities could be said to be somewhat similar to those proposed by the CMDC, given the central location of CMDC, unlike other UDC's. This gives the CMDC a role which it sees as concentrating on light commercial, residential, leisure and cultural development, rather than on the industrial development associated with the other UDC's. This is precisely the type of development that has been undertaken by the Toronto Harbourfront Corporation.

The role prescribed by the federal government for Harbourfront was the development of the Toronto waterline for the cultural/leisure benefit of Toronto residents. The Harbourfront, a federal crown corporation, has a series of powers viewed with suspicion by some in local politics, ie like CMDC it is not a democratically elected local organisation, and has a number of powers related to planning, compulsory purchase etc. However most would now concur that the role which it has developed and the development which it has produced on the waterline, does offer both Torontonians and tourists a series of opportunities which blend well with the work undertaken by the Toronto City

Council in this area of activity. The land on which Harbourfront operates is federal land. Some of this has been offered for lease, and some for sale by Harbourfront to private sector developers in specific areas of activity - hotels, retail, office and residential. Rents from leases are then used by Harbourfront to reinvest in cultural programmes. Consequently although Harbourfront has a different brief to the CMDC, in terms of the development that has taken place there, it does share some similar features to the CMDC.

The cultural facilities and animation programmes developed by Harbourfront include; a gallery of modern art, a dance studio, a cinema showing limited release film, a staged performances centre and an arts-in-education centre. In addition cultural animation is provided by a varied year round programme of festivals, workshops, literary readings and educational programmes.

*Boston, USA* is often cited as the city, par excellence, that has managed the economic miracle of urban regeneration by employing a strategy of both high technology and a commitment to the continued development of its arts and cultural industries. The most pertinent example of this commitment is its determination to create and extend its downtown cultural zone. The single, most powerful driving force in this is the City administration's decision to develop an Office of The Arts and Humanities, and this office's ability, through its commissioner, Bruce Rossley, to engage the support of other city departments in the establishment of the cultural zone. Within this zone a variety of districts have been established in order to provide for the "critical mass" of facilities and amenities necessary to create a cultural quarter. The formulation of a series of planning documents, and the creation of bye-laws and other legislation, allows for what one could term the most outrageous forms of "planning gain" to be obtained. A complex series of density bonuses, height bonuses, and other "incentives" ensure that little is built in the Boston downtown area which does not contribute to the city's plans for the creation of a series of arts facilities which range from development building of theatres, dance centres and other performing arts venues, through to the provision of affordable housing and studio workspace. In addition, a version of the "one per cent" scheme, and other planning controls, ensures that what building development does take place, does so according to the requirements of the arts and humanities office. As such, for example, in the cultural zone, all ground floors of buildings have to provide a percentage of "people friendly" facilities such as entertainments venues, restaurants, bars and "arts" related retail such as fashion stores, crafts, music and book shops.

The development of the cultural zone was initiated through an economic impact study, followed by vigorous advocacy of the economic benefits accruing from cultural development. Arts audits of both professional and voluntary organisations were undertaken, together with cultural consumption surveys of residents and tourists alike. In this way the arts and humanities commission was able to gain the support of the local community for its plans. Continuing advocacy of the economic benefits that the arts may bring is now held as received wisdom. For the Arts and Humanities Office, in the commissioners own words, "the advocacy battle has been won". As such, Boston is able to confidently proclaim its commitment to the arts, a factor which the City council sees as instrumental in making Boston a "people city". Although the public private partnership was perhaps initially an enforced affair, as far as the arts was concerned, Rossley now believes it is one in which both parties benefit. The extent to which this remains the case will be interesting to monitor, particularly the extent to which such partnerships are able to maintain sufficient support for the more experimental arts forms. While such experimentation may not be "good box-office" it should be recognised that such work is often both the forerunner of the more "accessible" art forms, and it provides a valuable "training ground" for later participation in the more accessible forms. Finally, it should be remembered that the "less accessible" art forms are of course, accessible to some, and are therefore as important to the communities that they serve, as are those forms which serve a wider set of interests.

Boston's experience is interesting because it provides what is possibly the most developed example of the ways in which the private sector has been harnessed to serve the interests of the arts community, and in turn, through the successful development of the cultural zone, the way in which the arts community has contributed to the success of the private sector. Such a relationship is particularly noticeable in the many shopping precincts where retail and arts entertainment and small cultural producers are combined, and where the demand for high cost residential facilities far exceeds supply. The success of Boston's stance however has been produced through the development of a comprehensive cultural plan advocated initially by the Office of the Arts and Humanities, but now perceived as received wisdom by all of the city council departments involved in its construction. It is doubtful whether such a unified cultural zone, and sufficiently concentrated critical mass could have been developed without: the integrated planning activities of the city council; the determination to adopt the planning legislation developed; the support obtained from both the public and arts associations involved.

In Britain, the inability of local government to raise taxes, such as tourist, sales and hotel taxes makes the creation of such cultural zones difficult. Nevertheless, attending to cultural planning by the adoption of strategies which integrate a variety of local authority departments including Leisure and Cultural Services, Economic Development, Planning and others, together with the knowledge base of arts organisations, could be an effective way of demonstrating a commitment to the arts and cultural industries which could allow for innovative development schemes involving the private sector in the development of cultural zones or quarters similar to that created in Boston.

*Dordrecht, The Netherlands:* Although very small, Dordrecht, as the oldest city in The Netherlands, possesses a number of features, museums, art galleries, and a number of buildings of architectural and historical interest which have led to plans to create a "cultural tourist zone" in the city centre.

Briefly, this zone will consist of a handbook guided, educational tour of the city centre's buildings having either architectural interest in their own right, or through acting as the location for what one might term Dordrecht's traditional "cultural artifacts". The city council is currently investigating ways in which local business, and arts organisations can contribute with the council in the creation of this zone. Although very different in scope and size to Boston's cultural zone, it shares the same attempt to create a "place" through the identification and central location of a set of fixed features. The construction of a passage through both time and space will be created by a physical tour of amenities, linked by a conceptual production of their relevance to the cultural tourist.

The recognition of the increasing importance of cultural tourism in Europe is the fundamental reasoning behind this development, and is obviously one strategy that can be relatively easily adopted by towns and cities with an architectural history and variety. Dordrecht's plans include the glazing and heating of some of the currently open spaces, together with the encouragement of small retail businesses that will reflect a sense of local pride in the centre's history. An added advantage of such schemes is that they are relatively inexpensive and easy to create, in that they require little infrastructure and building development, save for well sign-posted routes, and the production of suitable conceptual material, often available in great detail from voluntary associations specialising in local history and architecture. Additionally, because such routes are essentially conceptual constructions, ie a walk through a history which is invariably reconstructed, they allow for the creation of a variety of such cultural tours, and even provide for the creation of tours with competing interpretations. Such "play" with historical reality can produce challenging, if not discomforting reflections on the past.

Obviously, there are dangers associated with such proposals in that they involve a re-construction of a particular history. Second, they carry the danger of placing a particular 'culture' in a particular period, rather than encouraging the development of contemporary cultural life. Nevertheless, given the ability to mould such 'cultural tours' according to a variety of specifications they provide interesting and entertaining ways of 'discovering' a, rather than the, past.

While such strategies are one approach to the creation of cultural zones, we would guard against their overdevelopment, particularly in an area such as Greater Manchester which already has its' Castlefield, Lowry centre, Wigan Pier, Styal Mill and Clogs and Shawls canal trip, not to mention facilities such as the museum of working class history, and a number of other museums and art galleries. Rather than attempting to create yet more interpretive visions of heritage, we believe that a consideration of other, contemporary cultural forms would be more profitable for the creation of a cultural zone or quarter, and that the regions current artists, craftsmen and cultural producers are more worthy of consideration than those of the past, particularly so since the region has an international reputation for some of its current cultural activities in both "high" and "popular" culture.

*Rotterdam:* The major plans for cultural and tourism strategies in Rotterdam centre around its harbour, the worlds largest and busiest. Grontmij consulting engineers have produced a report for the Rotterdam Municipal Port Company which has investigated the tourist potential of the harbour. Similar, to the concerns of other cities, the plan is intended to encourage the growth of the cultural industries in the area which would also serve to promote the ports image and tourist potential and stimulate new investment and commercial enterprise. Grontmij's report recommends a joint approach to project development on the part of government and the commercial sector. The total investment costs are estimated at 12m guilders, (£3.5 - 4 million).

In addition to these proposals for the port itself, Rotterdam has also begun to develop the city's relationship with its river. An area designated "Water City" is in the process of development in Rotterdam. This is a mixed use development which contains residential, office, recreational/cultural, and small retail facilities. Currently there are approximately 1000 residential dwellings and plans are to increase this to 7,000 by 1995. Currently about 4500 people are working in offices in the area and plans are to increase this to 8000. Current recreational facilities include a history and maritime museum, an open air museum of historic vessels, and a crafts centre. Plans are to develop an art gallery and hotel, and to encourage the development of small retail facilities, bars and associated music clubs. The thematic cultural planning in which Rotterdam has engaged has enabled it to obtain significant central government funding. 10m guilders, (approximately £3 million) were recently obtained specifically for development projects in "Water City". The effects of some of this development for Rotterdam include the halting of long term migration from the city. Since 1981 the city has evidenced some demographic growth, reversing this long term trend.

The above examples provide for some international comparisons of regeneration schemes which have harnessed the arts and cultural industries in their development. In Great Britain we have examined developments in Glasgow, Scotland; Cardiff, Wales; Newcastle, Birmingham, Liverpool and Nottingham.

*Glasgow* is undoubtedly the city in Great Britain which is best known for its development of an arts directed urban regeneration strategy. This strategy has been so successful that, in 1987, it applied, and was awarded the title, European City of Culture, for the Year, 1990.

The strategy employed in Glasgow has required extensive support and cooperation from a variety of public and private sector organisations. These include, Glasgow District Council, The Greater Glasgow Tourist Board, Strathclyde Regional Council, The Scottish Development Agency, The Scottish Arts Council, and Glasgow Action. Glasgow Action, a public/private partnership was created to develop a strategy centred around: improving the city's image; developing the tourist industry; improving the city centre environment. With the support of the SDA and GDC, Glasgow Action began the rejuvenation of Merchant City, an inner city area, by promoting the development of residential property and "designer" retail outlets to form an embryonic cultural quarter. Other physical improvements in the inner city have also been undertaken by Glasgow Eastern Area Renewal, launched by the SDA in 1976. Since this time other physical improvements have been undertaken in partnership between the GDC and the SDA.

The major contribution of the arts to this regeneration process has been their harnessing to the development of the tourist industry strategy formulated by the GDC and GGTB. Glasgow's existing "high" culture assets, such as the Scottish Opera, Ballet and Orchestra, together with the BBC Scottish Symphony and Citizens theatre were marketed in a vigorous campaign and were added to with the opening of the Burrell Collection, and continued development of Mayfest, the annual arts festival.

In addition to the above the city has also developed a major national exhibition and conference centre, and the GDC and arts associations, with the support of the other organisations cited above have begun the development of cultural animation programmes throughout the summer months. These have included, international festivals of choral and folk music, jazz, dance and street theatre. All are vigorously marketed by the GGTB in an attempt to develop the city as a tourist destination, and with the announcement of the nomination as European City of Culture", the GDC established a Festivals Unit in order to coordinate a three year programme which will culminate in 1990. Since the origination of this tourist strategy the GDC has become the main actor in the arts led regeneration process, and has begun to develop a cultural policy to which other public and private funding bodies can respond.

With respect to the arts and cultural industries more specifically, one model which bears consideration is the Workshop and Artists Studio Provision Scotland Ltd (WASPS). Established in 1977, with the support of the Scottish Arts Council, this is a non-profit making company recognised a charity by the inland revenue. This company provides low cost and flexible rented accommodation to artist tenants together with a range of business services, including marketing, retail and gallery/exhibition services. The company currently has approximately 400 studios throughout Scotland in both urban and rural locations. Charges range from £10 - £15 for the average studio, and residential/studio combined space can be obtained for approximately £180 per month. The following are just two examples of workshop places available to artists in Glasgow.

*King Street, Glasgow* 62 studios ranging from 100 - 700 sq feet, occupying a total area of 20,000 sq feet on the third and fourth floors of a property owned by Glasgow District Council. Occupants include: painters, sculptors, designers, jewellers and stained glass artists.

*John Player Building, Alexandra Parade, Glasgow* 35,000 sq ft of accommodation for artists and craftspeople providing workshops, studios, offices and residential accommodation. The residential accommodation is reserved for artists from abroad wishing to live and work in Glasgow.

Similar schemes to the above exist in Toronto, Boston, New York and Cincinnati. In discussions with those responsible for the development of such schemes all stressed the importance of ensuring such provision in the inner urban areas in an attempt to ensure the maintenance of the artistic community. Such communities were seen as essential in promoting the inner city by helping provide a vitality associated with the artistic community. As such, such schemes should be viewed as part of the infrastructure development of inner city regeneration. In addition, given the avant garde nature of many of these organisations and their personnel, what others have called the new urban flanneurs, we would argue that such workspaces are ideal for location within cultural and entertainments quarters. They could be seen as a necessary part of such a quarter's infrastructure, as indeed they have become in those cities known for their cultural quarters, such as London, Paris, New York and Amsterdam.

However, there is already evidence to suggest that such organisations are having to leave city centre sites due to development. Such concern was the primary reason for the establishment of the Artspace organisation in Toronto detailed above. There is evidence that organisations and cultural producers in Manchester are also facing similar crises due to recent development, yet it is clear that such activity is often a major feature in the creation of a cultural ambience which in turn is itself attractive to developers. Consequently, it will be necessary to ensure that any proposals to develop such workspace cum arts centres, pay due attention to the affordability of such accommodation by the artistic community. It is precisely because of this that city's such as Toronto, Boston, New York, Minneapolis and others, have embarked upon low-cost or affordable residential and workplace schemes for their own artists and cultural producers. Importantly, such schemes are not only seen as public provision for the arts, but as a necessary financial investment in the cultural industries themselves and an investment attracting other industries and services. As such, in these cities the arts and cultural production has begun to serve as a major plank of urban regeneration.

*Sheffield:* In contrast to the cultural tourism and marketing initiatives which could be said to form the most important aspects of Glasgow's employment of the arts, Sheffield's response has focussed primarily on what one might term the post-electronic cultural industries, and popular cultural forms. In addition, unlike Glasgow's strategy which has incorporated strong associations between the public and private sector, Sheffield's response has been an initiative of local government, primarily the City Council's department of Employment and Economic Development. Rather than a desire to promote the city as a tourist destination, Sheffield's encouragement of the cultural industries was a response to recent large scale unemployment in its traditional industrial base.

Sheffield has created a cultural industries quarter in a previously declining area of the city, based on two main facilities; The Leadmill, and the Audio Visual Enterprise Centre (AVEC). The Leadmill opened in 1982 as a venue for rock bands and has now been expanded to incorporate on an adjoining site the AVEC which contains municipal recording studios and rehearsal facilities, a photographic gallery and workshop, Sheffield Independent Film, an association of film and video producers, two privately run recording studios owned by two of Sheffield's best known rock bands, and a small coffee bar cum eaterie. The council hopes to attract a variety of cultural producers to this area who will link with the adjacent science park and initiate research into the development of new technology in the audio-visual industries. The aim behind this cultural industries strategy is to encourage training, employment and small business development in this relatively new, and, in Sheffield, little developed economic sector.

A second initiative currently being developed in Sheffield is a cultural district in the centre of the city in Tudor Square. This cultural district will include the Crucible and Lyceum theatres, the Ruskin Crafts Gallery, the library, a new hotel and art gallery. The square is intended to become a focal point for arts events in the community. A final initiative, with a direct link to the arts, is the staging of the world student games in 1991 when a major youth oriented cultural festival will run alongside this international sporting event.

*Birmingham's* Media Quarter situated in the Digbeth area of the city is the main feature of its cultural industries strategy. The council have created a Media Development Agency, and intend to develop a Media Enterprise Centre in Digbeth.

A second strand to Birmingham's strategy is the creation of a series of cultural districts around the International Convention Centre, scheduled to open in 1991. The districts will each separately emphasise, theatre and entertainments, media, jewellry and Chinatown. These districts will be aimed at business tourists attracted to the Convention centre which includes conference facilities for up to 1500 delegates, and a concert hall for the Birmingham Symphony Orchestra. In addition to the convention centre, Birmingham plans to develop two National facilities, the National Aquarium, and the National Indoor Sports Arena. The development of a mixed use cultural district for festival shopping, a hotel, and office space, will, it is hoped, create a new image for Birmingham City Centre which will be marketed with a series of arts festivals in jazz, film and television.

*Liverpool:* Two distinct areas of activity can be discerned in Liverpool. The first relates to the activities of the Merseyside Development Corporation in the restoration of Albert Dock, the refurbishment of waterfront warehouses into a mixed use development with an arts component. This complex houses, the Tate Gallery of the North, the Maritime Museum, Granada TV's regional news centre, and a series of small shops, restaurants, offices and residential apartments.

The continued development of Albert Dock and a strengthening of links between it and the local authority and arts associations seems likely to develop now that the local authority has recognised that regeneration programmes such as this can be used to establish a foundation and provide confidence for further regeneration programmes in the city.

The second aspect to Liverpool's strategy for the arts and cultural industries lies in the emergence of an economic development framework for these, coupled with a city centre strategy. This strategy incorporates the creation of facilities for distribution, production, management and training in the arts and cultural industries. Developments underway include the creation of an agency for the local pop music industry, the appointment of a Film Liaison Officer, and a theatrical training scheme in association with the Everyman Theatre.

*Cardiff* claims to be the biggest broadcast production centre outside London, although we believe that much of this claim rests on its Welsh language broadcasting, given that it largely services the 22 hours per week of programming by S4C and is, therefore, less significant than might appear. Nevertheless, Cardiff is the main location for S4C, HTV and BBC Wales and over 5,000 people are employed in media-related jobs in South Glamorgan.

*Cardiff Media City* is an organisation sponsored by South Glamorgan's Economic Development Department to foster Cardiff's arts and cultural industries. It aims to bring together individuals and organisations for the purpose of mutual promotion and development, and to put those in need of these services in touch with those who can provide them.

A principal development of this organisation is the Media City Directory. This directory is essentially a trade directory which carries advertisements for Cardiff's cultural producers in the form of an alphabetically composed directory carrying a brief description of activities and services offered together with location details such as address, phone and fax. The directory is made up of six sections, namely; print, copy, centres, tv/film, theatres, and design. An introduction to the directory is provided which extols the virtues of Cardiff's arts and cultural industries. To describe the directory as a cultural industries 'Yellow Pages' would not really do justice to its Filofax production style, nevertheless, it is, in essence, precisely that.

The development of the Cardiff Media City Directory indicates a way in which a city can, with relatively little expense; promote its cultural industries, encourage cooperation between them, and provide a useful service to other economic sectors.

**Conclusion**

It can be seen from the above, at international, national and regional levels that the arts and cultural industries have a major role to play in the related areas of economic and urban regeneration. The cities and towns that we have examined are all engaged in a variety of programmes which have begun to treat the arts and cultural industries as an essential part of the urban and economic infrastructure. The following points summarise the nature of this treatment.

First the development of an integrated cultural policy by local authorities can set the agenda for future development. Second, these examples variously indicate the necessity of consultation with senior officers of arts organisations in the development of cultural policy. Such officers are invariably the most knowledgeable agents of arts and cultural production activities. Third, they provide examples of the role of economic development organisations in treating the arts and cultural production as an industry in its own right, and as an important contributor to the regional economy. Fourth, they show how cultural animation programmes, such as street theatre, busking, impromptu arts events and festival development can assist the establishment of cultural quarters. Fifth, they indicate how the establishment of cultural production facilities can become part of the infrastructure of urban regeneration. Finally, they contain examples of public-private partnerships of the widest possible base, necessary to ensure cooperation and support from the larger community in the creation of strategies to develop the arts and cultural industries.

# 8 The economics of the culture industry

*Howard Hughes and Chris Gratton*

## Introduction

The surveys undertaken as part of this study are reported below. We begin with an analysis of the responses to a questionnaire sent to cultural producers in the Greater Manchester region. This survey includes cultural producers acting in a variety of arts and cultural production activities, ranging from the larger producing and receiving theatres, dance, music, galleries and museums, through to those firms and individuals working in the audio-visual media, the record industry, craft and design. Importantly, this survey does not include the publishing industry. Initial attempts were made to develop an operational definition to include publishing, but our limited investigation of this industry failed to reveal any positive criteria upon which such a definition could be based.

Our surveys of arts consumers were undertaken at a series of venues, indicated in detail below. They included consumers of both "high art" and what one might term "popular culture".

We have attempted to employ methodologies similar to previous investigations elsewhere, but, as we indicate, such activity is fraught with difficulty, not least the different financial and time budgets with which these studies are undertaken. Nevertheless, we are confident that our figures do allow some general comparisons to be made.

## The Cultural Production Survey

A survey of organisations in the arts and cultural industries in the area was undertaken during July-August 1989. A small number of individuals - self-employed or small groups of people working together - was also surveyed. These individuals were mostly designers and craftspersons. Respondents to the survey are categorised in Table 1. (Note that the term individuals also includes small groups). Survey forms were returned by 72 organisations which covered, it is believed, most of the "significant" organisations in the area. The remaining forms were respondents in the individuals category. Clubs, discos, pubs, etc. which function as venues for entertainment and the arts were not surveyed but, undoubtedly, make a significant contribution to the economy of Greater Manchester. An estimate of their significance is included in table 15.

Organisations were most likely to be limited companies, with or without charitable status. Museums were mostly the responsibility of local government, with the others being trusts or companies with charitable status. Nearly two-thirds of the individuals were self-employed; the rest were partnerships, voluntary associations, co-operatives or companies.

*Findings*

Just over half (54%) of the respondents concentrated on one activity. For these who engaged in more than one activity the combination was usually the media arts and visual arts or drama and dance or design/craft and the visual arts.

Table 2 shows the length of time that respondents had been engaged in their artistic activities. A higher proportion of organisations than of individuals were well-established. the relatively high percentage of newcomers amongst individuals is perhaps a reflection of a rapid turnover in these sectors.

The survey also sought information about the premises used by the respondents for offices, for production, performing; display, workshop areas; and for rehearsal and storage. Not all respondents necessarily had a need for all three categories and others may have used the one premises for several purposes.

Those who owned all of their premises were the largest single group (see Table 3). Free use was the privilege of only 14.1%. Organisations were most likely to own or lease their premises with rehearsal/storage facilities being "free" to a significant number of theatres (17.4%) and museums/galleries (26.7%). Leasing of all facilities was most likely in the media arts sector (53.8%); leasing of all facilities was most likely in the media arts sector (53.8%); leasing by museums/galleries was uncommon. Use of part of own residence was colon amongst those in the visual arts (29.4%) and design/craft (39.1%).

The majority of respondents considered that their premises were adequate or very adequate (see Table 4.) This situation was reversed, however, for rehearsal/storage facilities; this aspect of dissatisfaction was apparent for nearly all categories or respondent. Museums and art galleries were generally more is-satisfied with their premises (of all forms) than were any other respondents.

With respect to staff changes, few of the respondents reported a reduction in staff employed since 1986. (See Table 5) Over a third reported an increase in staff with a further half reporting no change. Numbers of full time staff in museums and galleries had fluctuated most with a higher than average percentage reporting either a reduction or increase in staff. Museums and galleries had a large increase in part-time staff also. A higher than average percentage of media arts organisations reported an increase in full time staff as well as an increase in part time staff.

Over two thirds of respondents considered they were experiencing no recruitment problems and would not do so over the next two years. (See Table 6). Theatres were most likely to experience problems. Of those who did have or would face recruitment problems, 60.6% considered the problem to be a shortage of labour now and over the next two years. A similar proportion (57.1%) identified a lack of skills as the problem. Just over 48% considered that both problems were or would be present.

In the same way as a minority of respondents reported a reduction in staff since 1986, very few reported a fall in the volume of business over the same period (See Table 7). Most had increased their business and the proportion (59.3%) was higher than the proportion that had reported an increase in staff. Business had not expanded sufficiently to justify more staff and/or less labour intensive methods or production were being used.

A high proportion of the media arts respondents reported an increase in business and none reported a decrease. The overall financial position had worsened since 1986 for a minority of respondents (17.9%) (See Table 8). Despite the volume of business increasing in 59.3% of cases, the financial position had improved for only 41.9% (a reflection perhaps, or rising costs). It was the individuals who as a group had experienced the greatest fluctuations in fortunes. Only 37% of them had a stable financial position compared with 42.6% of the organisations.

The great majority of respondents had expansionist plans for the future (Table 9) and were optimistic that these plans could be realised. (See Table 10). Just over 80% aimed to increase the volume of business over the next two years and just over half aimed to increase the number of staff. This intended expansion was more evident in the case of organisations than for individuals. Media arts and museums, in particular, aimed to increase business and staff. Although respondents generally felt confident about achieving their aims, the level of confidence was less in respect of staff than of business volume. Media arts expressed the greatest levels of optimism and theatre and museums the least. Most respondents believed that their overall financial position would not worsen over the next two years (See Table 11). Forty per cent of museums and galleries felt that it would however. Quite a high percentage (42.5%) of all respondents felt they would have added other areas of activity to their current activity by 1991. This was especially so for media arts and invidious.

Respondents were asked to express their opinions about commercial lenders of finance. An overwhelming majority (86.5%) considered that such lenders were less aware of the nature and requirements of the arts and entertainment than they were of manufacturing industries. Under half

(44.1%) supported a plea for more favourable lending terms than those given to manufacturing; the majority (55.1%) asked for no more than equal terms. Nearly all (85.3%) considered availability of finance to be a serious constraint upon future development. It was, however, a less important constraint for individuals than for organisations.

Many respondents wished to see grants from public bodies and local authorities increase in importance as sources of their income over the next two years. (See Table 12). Many fewer, however, believed that this would actual occur. (Table 13). Media arts and individuals were least anxious to see increased income from public bodies and local authorities. Sponsorships were particularly desired by museums and galleries (76.5%); theatres also, though to a lesser extent (54.8%). Theatres were much keener than others to seek local authority support (83.9%). Museums were less keen to seek local authority support (52.9%) and many desired more public support (70.6%). Museums were very optimistic that sponsorship and grants from public bodies would increase (64.7%). there was, overall, a significant number of respondents who believed sponsorship would increase in importance. Most respondents expressed concern about the adequacy of funding over the next two years, and believed that neither trading sources nor sponsorship would prove adequate. (This clearly, was not the view of the media arts sector nor of the successful commercial theatre).

Three questions about income were aimed particularly at individuals. First, information was sought about the importance within total income of income from artistic activity. For nearly half, such income was 75% or more of total income (See Table 14). the overwhelming majority of respondents (85.7%) considered that their income from artistic activities was insufficient to give a "reasonable" living. (Those least dependent upon artistic income tended to be in the visual arts). For those who had been in business since 1986, artistic income had decreased in importance for only 14% and had actually increased within total income for nearly half (46.5%).

*Economic Impact*

The impact of the arts and cultural industries was assessed by using survey data, data from the Comedia report on the audio-visual economy in the North West (1988), and a variety of other sources for the information about "own-account artists and small companies".

Data from the survey was weighted and grossed up to give estimates for the entire arts and cultural industrial population. This is not identical with the methods used in the Myerscough report noted below and thus direct comparisons with Glasgow and Merseyside must be interpreted with caution.

Similar criteria for assessing impact are used here as were used in the Myerscough reports on Glasgow and Merseyside (1984-86). These latter were much more extensive investigations than was this investigation in Greater Manchester. Similar classifications and terminology have been used wherever possible; they differ from those used earlier in this survey report.

The turnover (or value of gross "output") in the Greater Manchester area is estimated at £343m (1988-89) (Table 15). A large part of this (approx 75%) is accounted for by broadcasting and, in particular, by Granada TV and BBC North

West; total turnover of these organisations is included as it has not been possible to estimate the percentage spent on "arts".

The audio-visual sector (excluding broadcasting) of the cultural industries is a considerable economic force (over £14m) within the total. There is a relationship between these audio-visual activities and broadcasting but to a degree they are "free-standing" and a function of local population, industry and commerce. Similarly the core organisations (Table 15) are related to a local market and it would appear that the turnover is considerable compared with Glasgow and Merseyside. This might be expected given the relative populations of the three areas (See Table 19) but the difference is also a reflection of "healthy" commercial theatre and venue activity as well as national and international status activity in the subsidised arts in Greater Manchester.

The income generated by core organisations turnover of £32.4m is estimated at £14.9m (See Table 16). Some of the turnover represents payments to other industries and thus does not create income directly in the arts and cultural industries. (The income that is created directly is approximately 0.40 of turnover). Some of this direct income is, in turn, re-spent and creates further income; a proportion of this re-spending is, however, "lost" out of Greater Manchester on purchases of goods and services from outside. The total effect is therefore less than if all responding had occurred within Greater Manchester. (The total income created is approx. 1.15 x the initial direct income).

Employment created by this economic activity is made up of a number of different categories of job. A total of 9100 jobs of all categories (without conversion to full-time equivalents) was generated in Greater Manchester. (See Table 17). Within the core organisations 60% of those jobs are full-time (Table 18). Male full time jobs outnumber female in all categories of core organisation by 6 to 1; for part time jobs the ratio is 1.3:1. Museums and galleries, however, have a much greater number of females working part time than they have males working part time. In the core organisations there is a large number of voluntary workers, equivalent to a further 30% of the existing employed labour force. the media arts sector provides more equal opportunities than the core organisations for female employment in that the number of full time female jobs is 80% of the number of male full time jobs.

In the same way that direct income created in the core organisations generates further income, so too do the direct jobs create further jobs. A further 1100 jobs are estimated to result from the direct jobs in the core organisations giving a total of 4000 jobs. Thus total jobs created are estimated at 102,000, equivalent to 1% of total employees in employment. (Merseyside 0.6%, Glasgow 1.1%). Further jobs will result from spending by arts consumers on non-arts goods and services, as well as from the multiplier effects of the own-account artists, small companies and the cultural industries effect similar to those of the core organisations discussed earlier.

**Cultural Production: Conclusion**

The cultural production survey reveals a sector of great diversity and one which is experiencing mixed fortunes. There are those who are faring well as commercial operations and face the future with considerable optimism; there are those whose financial position has become more precarious, particularly as "public sector" support has waned, and who face the future with much less optimism. Some of the major "institutions" of the area as well as a large number of individual artists, small ensembles and community arts ventures foresee difficult futures.

Overall there is a picture, however, which is reassuring in as much as business volumes have increased and are expected to continue increasing and in that for only a minority, financial positions ave worsened and are expected to worsen in the future. Staff numbers have increased and are expected to rise in the future for most of the sector.

There are, though, large numbers for whom the overall financial position has not improved and is not expected to improve in the near future. For most individuals, in particular, the artistic income they earn and on which they are heavily dependent, was deemed to be very inadequate. With respect to premises the most worrying aspect was inadequacy of rehearsal/storage facilities. Of concern also, is the perception that commercial lenders of finance lack understanding of the nature and needs of the arts. Although many in the arts (organisations in particular) wished to see more public body and local authority support, relatively few believed that this would occur. There was no suggestion that these in the arts wished to avoid a greater dependence upon "trading income", but the concern about adequacy of other sources reflects the peculiar nature of so much artistic activity that makes commercial operation often impractical and impossible. The arts and cultural industries are clearly a sector of economic significance in Greater Manchester, a sector comparable with those in other urban areas recently studied by Myerscough. Its turnover, excluding broadcasting but including the media arts of film, video, etc., is estimated at over £100 million and employment at over 6,500 jobs.

**Terms Used**

In the results of the survey respondents are classified as either organisations or individuals.

*"Organisations":*

1. The media arts of film, audio and video production (including the record industry).
2. Theatres and concerts which includes theatres, arts centres and performing organisations such as dance or drama companies or orchestras.
3. Museums and art galleries (but not commercial art galleries).

*"Individuals":*

those who are self-employed, free-lance, or work with a small number of others in the areas of dance, the visual arts, music, writing and design and craft. Includes free lance musicians and similar performing artists, ad-hoc professional groups, community arts, workshops and co-operatives.

Data was not collected in the survey about "performing artists" employed by organisations - actors, musicians, dancers, etc - except in so far as they were full time employees.

In the impact analysis terms similar to those used in the Myerscough reports are used, and differ slightly from those described above.

"Core Organisations": museums, art galleries, theatres and concerts, as specified above.

"Own Account artists and small companies ": as "individuals" above.

"Cultural industries": broadcasting, media arts (film, video, records) and cinema. Unlike the Myerscough reports it does not include publishing or the art trade.

**The Cultural Consumption Survey: Greater Manchester's Arts Customers and Their Spending**

This section of the report concentrates on the customers of Greater Manchester's arts organisations. Firstly we look at the profile of arts visitors based on our own customer survey over several of the region's arts attractions. Secondly we analyse the spending pattern of these customers and compare it with the national picture as revealed in Myerscough. Finally we assess the local economic impact of such consumer spending.

A customer survey was carried out at twelve arts venues, six of which were daytime attractions, the other six being evening performances. The daytime attractions were: the City Art Gallery, Castlefield, the Media Tour, the Manchester Museum, the Whitworth Art Gallery, and Wigan Pier. The evening attractions were the Royal Exchange, the Palace Theatre, the Library Theatre, Bolton Octagon, the Cornerhouse, and Band on the Wall. The daytime attractions correspond fairly closely to Myerscough's category of "Museums and galleries" for comparative purposes, whereas the evening attractions correspond to his category "Theatres and concerts".

Ideally, such a customer survey would be carried out over a considerable period of time covering attendances, in both winter and summer, over a wide variety of programmes offered by the arts organisations. Given the time and budget constraints, it was not possible to carry out such a comprehensive customer survey and the data relate to interviews carried out on a specific day, or at a specific performance, at each venue.

Such a procedure is unlikely to lead to serious bias in the data as regards the daytime attractions, but we are more concerned about the survey results as regards the evening attractions. For the latter, different programmes may well attract different audience profiles (in particular at the theatre venues) and we would argue that the results for the evening attractions should be regarded more as a pilot for a much more comprehensive survey.

There is a further problem with interviews at the evening attractions. At evening performances, due to the difficulty of interviewing respondents as they enter or leave a theatre or concert, subsequent telephone interviews were carried out with those respondents that agreed to leave their name and telephone number when contact was made at the venue. Although such a procedure substantially improves the quality of the data from those interviews completed, there are difficulties in following up overnight tourists. Consequently very few tourists appear in the sample for evening attractions and no data is presented separately for this category since the sample is too small to be viable. Also, the procedure led to less than viable sample sizes for both the Palace and the Library Theatre and although respondents from these venues appear in the aggregate figures, they are not picked out separately in the venue by venue analysis.

*Findings: Profile of Arts Visitors in Greater Manchester*

In total 420 interviews were carried out at the twelve arts/visitor attractions. 47 per cent of respondents were female and 53 per cent were male. Half the respondents were in the 20-39 age category with a further 33 per cent coming from the 40-59 age category.

Table 1 shows that arts visitors are predominantly from the higher socioeconomic groups. 39 per cent of respondents were from managerial and professional occupational groups (AB). This group made up over 50 per cent of the sample at Castlefield, the Royal Exchange and the Band on the Wall. The next most important group in terms of numbers was students. Students were the most important category at the City Art Gallery, the Manchester Museum, and the Cornerhouse (where they represented 45 per cent of the sample). The third significant group of arts visitors were the C1's (Admin and Clerical) who were particularly well represented at the Cornerhouse (24 per cent of sample) and the Band on the wall (28 per cent)

Table 2 shows the area of residence of arts visitors. Overall 49 per cent of visitors lived in the Greater Manchester area, 44 per cent in other areas of the UK, and 7 per cent were from abroad, but there was significant variation in these proportions from venue to venue.

The Daytime Venues fell into two categories. Castlefield, the Media Tour, and Wigan Pier attract most of their visitors from outside Greater Manchester. The City Art Gallery, Manchester Museum, and Whitworth Art Gallery are catering mainly, though not exclusively, to Greater Manchester residents. However all the Daytime Venues attract a significant number of visitors from outside the area. Castlefield attracted the highest proportion (21 per cent) of visitors from abroad. The Media Tour attracted the highest proportion (88 per cent) of visitors from outside the Greater Manchester area.

In contrast, the evening venues appear to attract a higher proportion of Greater Manchester residents although 42 per cent of Royal Exchange visitors and 34 per cent of Band on the Wall visitors were from outside the Greater

Manchester area. The lack of many visitors from abroad in the sample from the evening audiences may be due to the sampling bias referred to earlier.

Table 3 shows how frequently respondents visited the venue at which they were interviewed. Again there is a sharp contrast in visitor profile between Daytime and Evening Venues, with the former attracting a much higher proportion of first time visitors. Equally, within the group of Daytime Venues, there is a sharp contrast between City Art Gallery, Whitworth Art Gallery, and Manchester Museum on the one hand, and Castlefield, the Media Tour, and Wigan Pier on the other, with the latter group attracting a higher proportion of first time visitors. Both the Royal Exchange and the Cornerhouse have 58 per cent of their customers visiting at least once per month. The Band on the Wall also has a high proportion of regular visitors. Bolton Octagon is unusual amongst the Evening Venues in having both a low proportion of first time visitors and a low proportion of regular visitors.

Table 4 shows how frequently respondents visited other arts attractions in the Greater Manchester area. In general, respondents from Evening Venues were more likely to visit other arts attractions more frequently than those interviewed at Daytime Venues. The Media Tour was exceptional in that 69 per cent of respondents interviewed visited other arts attractions in Manchester less than once a year. This probably reflects the high proportion of visitors to the Media tour that were from outside the Greater Manchester area. 23 per cent of visitors to Daytime Venues stayed overnight in the Greater Manchester area (see Table 5), with roughly half those staying in hotels or guest houses and the other half staying with family and friends. Perhaps surprisingly, the smallest proportion staying overnight out of the six daytime attractions were from visitors to the Media tour. On the other hand, of those that did stay overnight, the Media Tour visitors had the highest proportion staying in hotels and guesthouses. Out of the sample of visitors to Evening Venues only four stayed overnight (1 in hotel, 3 with friends). Again this lack of overnight stays associated with evening visits to arts attractions could be due to the survey method employed.

Table 6 gives an indication of the percentage of respondents spending money on other leisure activities in Greater Manchester on the same day as the visit to the arts attraction. The most common ancillary expenditure (68 per cent of respondents), in addition to entry prices and programmes etc, was on drinks at the venue, followed by (41 per cent) drinks purchased elsewhere in Greater Manchester. There is a clear distinction between daytime and evening visitors when it comes to other categories of ancillary expenditures. Whereas a high proportion of daytime visitors spend money on meals in Greater Manchester's restaurants, on other leisure attractions and on shopping, very few visitors to evening attractions spend money on these items.

This distinction is present again in Table 7, which looks at the percentage for whom the visit to venue was the main reason for the visit to Greater Manchester. For nearly all evening visitors, the arts attraction was the main reason for the visit. This is true also for Castlefield and the Media Tour, and a majority of Wigan Pier visitors regarded the attraction as the main reason for the visit to Greater Manchester. However only a minority of visitors to Manchester Museum and the City and Whitworth Art Galleries came mainly to visit these arts attractions.

Table 8 shows that the main method of transport to virtually all the venues was the car, accounting for about a half of all visits. The exception was Bolton Octagon where the coach was the main method of travel, but again this probably reflects the weakness of interviewing only on one evening (which may have exceptionally included a large number of respondents travelling on a coach). Coach travel is, not surprisingly, also important for Castlefield, the Media Tour, and Wigan Pier.

Overall, the data in this section indicates that, from our sample of Greater Manchester arts attractions, it is the daytime attractions that bring in more visitors from outside the region, result in the more overnight stays, and generate a wider range of ancillary expenditures than Evening Attractions. Amongst the daytime attractions, Castlefield, the Media Tour, and Wigan Pier are particularly important in respect of such effects. However in terms of the economic impact of visitor expenditure it is not only the number of visitors spending money on various items in Greater Manchester that is important, but also the amount of money they spend. It is to this topic we now turn.

*Spending by Arts Customers in Greater Manchester*

The average amounts spent by different types of arts customer is broken down by different categories of expenditure, is given in Table 9. National averages for the same categories of expenditure appear in Table 10, these 'national averages' being Myerscough's estimates based on survey work in Merseyside, Glasgow, and Ipswich.

In general the national pattern of expenditure by different types of visitor is reflected in the region: Tourists in total spent more than Day Visitors who in turn spent more than Residents. Tourists spent a lot more than other visitors on shopping and other items outside the arts venue as well as on accommodation. Similarly, Day Visitors spent more on out-of-venue expenditures than Residents although they also spent most on items consumed within the venue (again this pattern exactly reflects the national picture). Where our data differs markedly from the "national data" is in the expenditure of visitors to Theatres and Concerts (ie evening visitors). In particular, among these visitors expenditure on shopping and other items in Greater Manchester is virtually non existent. Also, since there were few overnight stays associated with these visits, the expenditure of Tourists to Theatres and Concerts does not appear at all. Again, the message here seems to be that a much more detailed survey is necessary of evening visitors to Greater Manchester's arts attractions.

If we ignore evening visitors to Theatres and Concerts, expenditure by visitors to the region's arts attractions are substantially above those revealed in Myerscough (over 50 per cent higher). Part of this is due to inflation between 1985/86 when the Myerscough survey work was done and 1989 when our customer survey was carried out. However, inflation would account for less than half the increase in expenditure by arts visitors in Manchester compared with Myerscough's survey. It seems that the specific daytime attractions included in our survey have much higher levels of arts related expenditure than would be the case in other cities outside London.

*Economic Impact*

Economic impact analysis requires the assessment of how much of the spending of arts customers in Greater Manchester converts into increased local income, and hence jobs, in the area. The spending of visitors at the arts venue has already been included in the economic impact calculations of Section 8a since all this expenditure is included in the turnover estimates in that Section. In this section we therefore concentrate on the economic impact of spending by arts customers outside the venue.

The overall aim of the economic impact analysis is to estimate the loss to local income that would result if the arts sector were to cease to operate. In earlier economic impact studies it was reasonable to assume that all income generated by visitors from outside the area was a net addition to economic activity in the local economy. Income generated by the spending of local residents is more difficult to deal with. It is possible that such spending would have taken place anyway in the local area and therefore it would not have represented a net addition to economic activity.

However, in the national study (Myerscough) detailed survey work showed that expenditure by arts visitors from the local area did not represent 'deadweight' expenditure (ie not contributing anything extra to the local economy). It was found that only 10 per cent of the arts-related expenditure of local residents was not specifically attributed to the arts. That is, if the arts contributions were not in existence, there was evidence that 90 per cent of arts related expenditure would not have been spent in the local economy. The study also found that not all day-visitor arts related expenditure was not specifically attributable to the arts but only 91 per cent of it.

The method employed to gauge the economic impact of the arts on Greater Manchester involves estimating the spending of both arts institutions and its customers. The former has been carried out in Section 8a and here we will concentrate on the latter. In particular we will restrict ourselves to customers of Theatres and Concerts and Museums and Galleries since the other major sector, Cultural Industries, are unlikely to generate a similar customer affect.

Spending outside the venues is aggregated up to give a total figure for Greater Manchester (using turnover figures from the production survey). This total is then adjusted to allow for 'deadweight' expenditure. This arts related expenditure by arts customers then makes up total, direct expenditure by arts customers. This direct arts expenditure can then be converted into local income and jobs in a similar fashion to used in the analysis of the production survey.

However the rate of impact of spending by arts customers is much lower than for spending by arts organisations because a smaller proportion of spending by businesses such as shops and restaurants is paid to local employees as wages and salaries. Hence the local income and jobs generated by £100,000 of customer spending is less than that generated by £100,000 spending by an arts organisation. On the other hand, the actual amounts spent by arts customers to Theatres and Concerts and Museums and Galleries is much greater than the total amount spent by the arts organisations in these categories. Hence the total impact of customer spending is higher than that for these arts organisations.

Total customer spending in Greater Manchester is estimated at £87.4 million in 1989. This is estimated to generate £17.68 million of local income to the Greater Manchester area and 5,324 jobs.

### Cultural Consumption: Conclusion

Arts organisations in Greater Manchester make a substantial contribution to the local economy both in terms of their own spending and that of their customers. In total, the local income (and local jobs) generated by customer spending is greater than that generated by the turnover of the core organisations in the Museums and Galleries and Theatres and Concerts categories. The overall turnover of £32.4 million of the core organisations in these categories generates a further £84.7 million of customer spending.

Greater Manchester is therefore already well adapted to generating economic activity through the spending of its arts customers. Arts acts as a magnet to draw people to the city and their expenditure then generates additional local income and jobs. The more the region can attract visitors from outside the local area, and in particular tourists who stay overnight, then the greater the economic impact of arts customer spending will be.

# Appendix I
# Cultural production tables

*Howard Hughes*

Table 1
Primary activity of respondents

| | |
|---|---|
| Organisations: | %age |
| Media arts | 11.3 |
| Theatre and concerts | 25.0 |
| Museums and galleries | 13.7 |
| Individuals: | |
| Dance | -3.2 |
| Visual arts | 13.7 |
| Music | -8.9 |
| Literary | -1.6 |
| Design/craft | 20.2 |
| other | -2.4 |

Table 2
Number of years involved with the arts

| | Organisations %age | Individuals %age |
|---|---|---|
| 10 years or over | 70 | 33.3 |
| 5-9 years | 20 | 30.0 |
| 2-4 years | -8.3 | 16.7 |
| less than 2 years | -1.7 | 20 |

Table 3
Premises: own, lease or free use

| | %age |
|---|---|
| own all | 42.2 |
| lease all | 29.7 |
| free use of all | 14.1 |

Table 4
Adequacy of premises

| | offices | work/production performing area | rehearsal storage |
|---|---|---|---|
| | %age | %age | %age |
| very adequate | 13.8 | 17.3 | -6.7 |
| adequate | 56.0 | 57.7 | 38.5 |
| not adequate | 30.2 | 25.0 | 54.8 |

Table 5
Changes in staff since 1986

| | full-time %age | part-time %age | short-term contract %age | gov't training schemes %age | casual %age | volunteers %age |
|---|---|---|---|---|---|---|
| increase | 34.7 | 38.0 | 34.6 | 36.4 | 24.5 | 36.1 |
| constant | 48.0 | 52.0 | 50.0 | 40.9 | 62.1 | 58.3 |
| decrease | 17.3 | 10.0 | 15.4 | 22.7 | -3.4 | -5.6 |

Table 6
Staff recruitment problems

| | organisations %age | individuals %age |
|---|---|---|
| no problems now or foreseen | 68.6 | 67.4 |
| problems currently | -1.9 | -2.2 |
| problems in next 2 years | -5.9 | -2.2 |
| problems currently & in next 2 years | 23.6 | 28.2 |

Table 7
Change in volume of business since 1986

| | organisations %age | individuals %age |
|---|---|---|
| increased | 61.3 | 57.4 |
| constant | 27.4 | 31.5 |
| decreased | 11.3 | 11.1 |

Table 8
Change in overall financial position since 1986

| | organisations %age | individuals %age |
|---|---|---|
| improved | 37.7 | 46.3 |
| remained stable | 42.6 | 37.0 |
| worsened | 19.7 | 16.7 |

Table 9

Aims up to 1991

| | volume of business | | number of staff | |
|---|---|---|---|---|
| | organisations | individuals | organisations | individuals |
| | %age | %age | %age | %age |
| increase | 87.1 | 75.0 | 63.6 | 43.0 |
| maintain | 12.9 | 21.7 | 36.4 | 54.7 |
| decrease | - | -3.3 | - | -1.9 |

Table 10

Level of optimism about achieving aims

| | volume of business | | number of staff | |
|---|---|---|---|---|
| | organisations | individuals | organisations | individuals |
| | %age | %age | %age | %age |
| very optimistic | 29.5 | 23.2 | 18.5 | 31.9 |
| moderately optimistic | 27.9 | 17.8 | 22.2 | -8.5 |
| optimistic | 16.4 | 30.4 | 25.9 | 21.3 |
| optimistic with reservations | 26.2 | 25.0 | 25.9 | 34.0 |
| not optimistic | - | -3.6 | -7.5 | -2.3 |

Table 11

Forecast of overall financial position by 1991

| | organisations | individuals |
|---|---|---|
| | %age | %age |
| improve | 36.2 | 54.2 |
| be stable | 43.1 | 35.6 |
| worsen | 20.7 | 10.2 |

Table 12

Desire to see certain sources of income increase in importance in the future

| | organisations | individuals |
|---|---|---|
| | %age | %age |
| box office revenue; sales;fees; commissions etc. | 84.9 | 87.2 |
| other trading income | 30.6 | 27.4 |
| donations (private) | 22.6 | -9.7 |
| grants from public bodies | 54.8 | 33.9 |
| grants from Local Authorities | 58.1 | 33.9 |
| sponsorship | 50.0 | 33.9 |

Table 13
Belief that certain sources of income will increase in importance in future

| | organisations %age | individuals %age |
|---|---|---|
| box office revenue; sales;fees; commissions etc. | 88.9 | 83.6 |
| other trading income | 46.8 | 19.3 |
| donations (private) | 17.7 | -8.1 |
| grants from public bodies | 24.2 | 19.3 |
| grants from Local Authorities | 17.7 | 19.3 |
| sponsorship | 50.0 | 25.8 |

Table 14
Importance within total income of income from artistic activity (individuals only)

| | %age |
|---|---|
| Less than 20% | 29.3 |
| 20% - 59% | 19.5 |
| 60% - 74% | -4.9 |
| 75% or more | 46.3 |

Table 15
Turnover of the arts and cultural industries (£m)

| | Greater M/C | Merseyside | Glasgow |
|---|---|---|---|
| Core organisations | | | |
| Museums & galleries | -8.5 | -7.23 | -7.77 |
| Theatres & concerts | 23.9 | -6.80 | 17.70 |
| Own account artists & small companies | -5.9 | -3.1 | -4.9 |
| Cultural industries | 304.92 | -6.7 | 173.7 |
| Total | 343.22 | -23.83 | 204.1 |

*(Note data for Greater Manchester relates to 1988 -89 for Glasgow & Merseyside it relates to 1984 - 86.)*

Table 16

Value-added by the arts & cultural industries (£m) core-organisations only

| | Greater M/C | Merseyside | Glasgow |
|---|---|---|---|
| Direct income generated by turnover | 12.96 | -5.67 | -9.59 |
| Total income generated within the area by turnover | 14.90 | -6.37 | 11.4 |

Table 17

Employment in arts and cultural industries

| | Greater M/C | Merseyside | Glasgow |
|---|---|---|---|
| Direct jobs (all categories) in: | | | |
| Core organisations: | | | |
| Museums & galleries | -700 | 737 | -675 |
| Theatres & concerts | 2200 | 589 | 1587 |
| Own account artist's & small companies | -900 | -806 | -762 |
| Cultural industries | 5300 | -412 | 5493 |
| Total | 9100 | 2544 | 8517 |
| Total jobs (all categories) generated by core organisations | 4000 | 1698 | 2620 |

Table 18

Categories of employment in the core organisations

Museums, galleries, theatres & concerts in Greater Manchester

| | %age |
|---|---|
| Full-time | 60.0 |
| Part-time | 22.4 |
| Casual | -7.3 |
| Govt. Training | -7.0 |
| Short-term contract | -3.3 |

Table 19
Background data

| | Greater M/C | Merseyside | Glasgow |
|---|---|---|---|
| Population (1985-86) | 2.6m | 1.5m | 1.6m |
| Employees in employment | 0.98m | 0.50m | 0.83m * |
| Unemployment (Oct 1988) | 0.12m | 0.10m | 0.15m * |
| GDP per head (£ 1984) | £4365 | £3955 | £4063 * |

** figures relate to Strathclyde. The Myerscough study covered an area greater than Glasgow city but less than Strathclyde*

Table 20
Percentage of income derived from various sources

| | local authorities %age | public bodies %age | sponsorship donations %age |
|---|---|---|---|
| Media Arts | -1.1 | -2.9 | -0.9 |
| Dance | 27.0 | -9.1 | -0.8 |
| Visual Arts | -9.8 | 21.3 | -1.4 |
| Theatre | 15.5 | 12.5 | -1.1 |
| Music | -2.5 | -3.7 | -0.2 |
| Design/Crafts | - | -0.2 | - |
| Museums/Heritage | -6.9 | 38.9 | -5.2 |
| Other | 62.6 | 1.3 | - |

*Above percentages are percentage of total income of each category of activity. i.e. 1.1% of the income of the media arts is derived from local authorities.*

# Appendix II
# Cultural consumption tables

*Chris Gratton*

Table 1
Occupational groupings of arts visitors to Manchester

| | %age |
|---|---|
| AB Managerial & Professional | 39 |
| C1 Admin & Clerical | 16 |
| C2 Skilled Manual | -8 |
| D Semi & Unskilled Manual | -3 |
| E Pensioner/Retired | -9 |
| Housewife | -6 |
| Student | 17 |
| Unemployed | -3 |

Table 2
Area of residence of arts visitors to Manchester

| | Visitor Lives In Greater Manchester %age | Elsewhere in UK %age | Abroad %age |
|---|---|---|---|
| Daytime Venues: | | | |
| City Art Gallery | 49 | 33 | 18 |
| Castlefield | 30 | 49 | 21 |
| Media Tour | 12 | 78 | 10 |
| Manchester Museum | 61 | 21 | 18 |
| Whitworth Art Gallery | 60 | 34 | -6 |
| Wigan Pier | 27 | 71 | -2 |
| Evening Venues: | | | |
| Royal Exchange | 58 | 42 | - |
| Bolton Octagon | 73 | 27 | - |
| Cornerhouse | 84 | 16 | - |
| Band On The Wall | 66 | 34 | - |
| Total | 49 | 44 | -7 |

Table 3
Frequency of visit to main venue

| | first visit %age | once /Mth %age | every 3 Mth %age | every 6Mth %age | once /yr %age | less than once yr %age |
|---|---|---|---|---|---|---|
| Daytime Venues: | | | | | | |
| City Art Gallery | 34 | 21 | 12 | -9 | 15 | -9 |
| Castlefield | 59 | -2 | -7 | -9 | 18 | -5 |

| | | | | | | |
|---|---|---|---|---|---|---|
| Media Tour | 94 | -2 | -2 | - | -2 | - |
| Manchester Museum | 40 | 12 | -9 | 12 | -6 | 21 |
| Whitworth Art Gallery | 37 | 17 | 17 | 15 | 14 | - |
| Wigan Pier | 60 | -4 | -8 | -8 | 10 | 10 |
| Evening Venues: | | | | | | |
| Royal Exchange | 15 | 58 | 20 | -7 | - | - |
| Bolton Octagon | -7 | -7 | -7 | 36 | 14 | 29 |
| Cornerhouse | -5 | 58 | 29 | -5 | -3 | - |
| Band On The Wall | 22 | 31 | 16 | 13 | -9 | -9 |
| Total | 38 | 22 | 14 | 11 | -8 | -7 |

Table 4
Frequency of visit to other venues

| | once /Mth %age | every 3 Mth %age | every 6Mth %age | once /yr %age | less than once yr %age |
|---|---|---|---|---|---|
| Daytime Venues: | | | | | |
| City Art Gallery | 27 | 24 | 12 | -6 | 30 |
| Castlefield | 13 | 26 | 21 | -8 | 33 |
| Media Tour | 12 | -8 | -8 | -4 | 69 |
| Manchester Museum | 33 | -6 | 21 | -9 | 30 |
| Whitworth Art Gallery | 29 | -9 | 17 | 14 | 31 |
| Wigan Pier | 20 | 12 | 16 | 12 | 37 |
| Evening Venues: | | | | | |
| Royal Exchange | 30 | 22 | 25 | -2 | 22 |
| Bolton Octagon | 46 | 36 | 11 | -7 | - |
| Cornerhouse | 64 | 13 | 18 | -5 | - |
| Band On The Wall | 53 | -9 | 16 | - | 22 |
| Total | 31 | 16 | 17 | -6 | 29 |

Table 5
Percentage staying overnight and type of accommodation

| | %age staying overnight %age | of which %age staying: i) with family or friends %age | ii) in hotels or guesthouses %age |
|---|---|---|---|
| Daytime Venues Only: | | | |
| City Art Gallery | 33 | 55 | 45 |
| Castlefield | 23 | 67 | 33 |
| Media Tour | 14 | 23 | 77 |

| | | | |
|---|---|---|---|
| Manchester Museum | 28 | 50 | 50 |
| Whitworth Art Gallery | 23 | 57 | 43 |
| Wigan Pier | 25 | 64 | 36 |
| | | | |
| Total | 23 | 52 | 48 |

Table 6

%age of persons spending money on other activities in Greater Manchester

| | meal at venue %age | meal in GM %age | drink at venue %age | drink in GM %age | shopping in GM %age |
|---|---|---|---|---|---|
| Visited Attraction Daytime Venues: | | | | | |
| City Art Gallery | -3 | 58 | - | 82 | 72 |
| Castlefield | 50 | 46 | 82 | 61 | 39 |
| Media Tour | 82 | 48 | 98 | 65 | 45 |
| Manchester Museum | -3 | 67 | -9 | 70 | 75 |
| Whitworth Art Gallery | 31 | 49 | 57 | 71 | 47 |
| Wigan Pier | 20 | 12 | 16 | 12 | 37 |
| Visited Attraction Evening Venues: | | | | | |
| Royal Exchange | 23 | 17 | 73 | 27 | 17 |
| Bolton Octagon | - | -7 | 71 | 11 | - |
| Cornerhouse | 11 | -8 | 50 | 34 | - |
| Band On The Wall | 22 | 13 | 100 | 50 | - |
| | | | | | |
| Total | 32 | 32 | 68 | 48 | 33 |

Table 7

%age for whom visit to venue was main reason for visit

| | %age |
|---|---|
| Daytime Venues: | |
| City Art Gallery | 38 |
| Castlefield | 80 |
| Media Tour | 80 |
| Manchester Museum | 42 |
| Whitworth Art Gallery | 38 |
| Wigan Pier | 58 |
| Evening Venues: | |
| Royal Exchange | 89 |
| Bolton Octagon | 100 |

| | |
|---|---|
| Cornerhouse | 100 |
| Band On The Wall | 97 |
| | |
| Total | 74 |

Table 8
Method of travel to venue

| | walk %age | train %age | car %age | coach %age | bus %age | other %age |
|---|---|---|---|---|---|---|
| Daytime Venues: | | | | | | |
| City Art Gallery | -6 | 18 | 36 | - | 36 | -3 |
| Castlefield | -5 | 21 | 49 | 12 | 14 | - |
| Media Tour | -2 | 12 | 47 | 33 | -6 | - |
| Manchester Museum | 18 | -3 | 49 | - | 30 | - |
| Whitworth Art Gallery | 23 | -9 | 34 | -6 | 26 | -3 |
| Wigan Pier | -4 | -6 | 65 | 12 | -8 | -4 |
| Evening Venues: | | | | | | |
| Royal Exchange | -7 | 12 | 70 | - | 12 | - |
| Bolton Octagon | -4 | -4 | 18 | 68 | - | -7 |
| Cornerhouse | - | 11 | 55 | - | 24 | 11 |
| Band On The Wall | 13 | 13 | 50 | - | 25 | - |
| Total | -7 | 11 | 49 | 13 | 18 | -3 |

Table 9
Spending by arts customers in Greater Manchester:
average spend per person per visit (£'s)

| Total: | in venue (tickets refresh-ments etc) | food drink in GM | travel in GM | other in GM | acc md atn |
|---|---|---|---|---|---|
| Residents: | | | | | |
| Museums & Galleries £14.81 | 4.34 | 4.51 | 1.39 | 4.57 | - |
| Theatres & Concerts £9.88 | 6.79 | 1.21 | 1.83 | 0.05 | - |
| Day Visitors: | | | | | |
| Museums & Galleries £19.65 | 8.07 | 3.50 | 1.83 | 6.25 | - |

| | | | | | |
|---|---|---|---|---|---|
| Theatres & Concerts £12.29 | 7.82 | 2.41 | 2.06 | - | - |
| Tourists: | | | | | |
| Museums & Galleries £40.67 | 6.79 | 6.38 | 3.90 | 17.29 | 6.31 |

Table 10
Spending by arts customers "nationally"
average spend per person per visit (£'s)

| | in venue (tickets refresh-ments) | food drink | travel | other | acc md atn |
|---|---|---|---|---|---|
| Total: | | | | | |
| Residents: | | | | | |
| Museums & Galleries | 1.49 | 1.34 | 1.02 | 5.28 | - |
| Theatres & Concerts | 5.20 | 1.52 | 1.05 | 1.82 | - |
| Day Visitors: | | | | | |
| Museums & Galleries | 2.53 | 2.56 | 1.84 | 6.31 | - |
| Theatres & Concerts | 8.11 | 1.97 | 1.74 | 1.68 | - |
| Tourists: | | | | | |
| All | 2.48 | 4.47 | 1.46 | 8.77 | 10.3 |

Source: Myerscough 1987
NB: "National" averages are in fact based on the averages for Glasgow, Merseyside and Ipswich.

